31 Christmas Devotional
DAYS WITH BETHLEHEM'S TREASURE
Volume 2

SHANE JOHNSON

31 DAYS WITH BETHLEHEM'S TREASURE
By: Shane Johnson
Copyright © 2016
GOSPEL FOLIO PRESS
All Rights Reserved

Published by
GOSPEL FOLIO PRESS
304 Killaly St. W.
Port Colborne, ON L3K 6A6
CANADA

ISBN: 9781927521922

Cover design by Danielle Robins

All Scripture quotations from the
King James Version unless otherwise noted.

Printed in the United States of America

Foreword

While not all Canadians enjoy the cold, most look forward to the Christmas season. People enjoy sparkling lights in the snow, cozy family time protected from the cold, Christmas music, baking and a myriad of other Christmas traditions. One of my favourite customs in December is reading *31 Days at Bethlehem's Manger*, the first Christmas devotional from Shane Johnson.

Over the years I've realized how absolutely crazy the Christmas season can become. As a child there is a Christmas program to participate in, a gift or two bought for mom and dad, and attending family events. The full realization of what had to happen for different events doesn't sink in until you've helped out or organized something yourself. It is easy to get overwhelmed by the planning, spending, shopping, cooking, baking, running around, and general preparations.

Often we are told to remember what we are celebrating, but do we take quality time to do so? We enjoy Christmas themed messages on Sundays, but is that where it ends? The verse in Luke often comes to mind, *"For where your treasure is, there will your heart be also"* (Luke 12:34). How I spend my time is often a good representation of where I'm laying up treasure. *31 Days at Bethlehem's Manger* has been such a blessing for me in the midst of the busyness of Christmas. It forces (yes, forces) me to be still and reflect on the significance of the holiday. Every morning and evening can be spent meditating on different aspects of the Lord's coming. Each piece of this historical event has significance we may not otherwise spend time thinking about. Christmas is not just about the baby who came, but about the Man who died in my place. Shane celebrates the baby's coming while pointing to His ultimate victory over sin. I look forward to adding these devotional thoughts to my day to re-focus on what Christ has done for me.

That if thou shalt confess with thy mouth the Lord Jesus, and shalt believe in thine heart that God hath raised him from the dead, thou shalt be saved.
Romans 10:9

To God be the glory,
Danielle Robins
September 2016

December 1

"Behold, I come, in the scroll of the book it is written of Me."   Psalm 40:7, NKJV

In 1969, Neil Armstrong stepped out of a lunar module and placed a human foot for the first time ever on the moon. He went down in history as saying, "That's one small step for man; one giant leap for mankind." Never before had mankind reached such a milestone in space exploration. For the first time ever we had breached the lunar world. We had come a long, long way.

God had come a long way, too. Stepping out of His own lunar module called Mary's womb, after taking His first look at planet Earth, He too could say, "That's one small step for God, one infant step, but one giant leap for mankind." That one small step jumped the galaxies in order to breach one giant divide. Timely and eternal, small and colossal, that one infant step provided the only Mediator for all mankind. That "one small child in a land of a thousand" bridged a chasm so vast no mere human being could ever have hoped to cross it alone. That one small step forever forged a union of fragile humanity with iron divinity, creating a God-Man who would totally obliterate the sins of this world. "Oh, the mighty gulf that God did span at Calvary" (*At Calvary*, William Reed Newell).

But that first manger step was only the beginning of a long journey that lay ahead of Him. After a brief stay in Bethlehem, the little Saviour travelled to Egypt to escape the first of the hostilities He faced on this planet, for the power hungry Herod killed every infant in Bethlehem in a vain attempt to kill Him. Then for thirty years He lived in Nazareth working as a humble carpenter, though He was the architect of the whole planet. He served in the local synagogue in appearance as a worshipper, but in reality the object of their worship.

Lastly, His journey took Him through the streets and hamlets of Galilee, unknown to men but known and adored by all heaven. At the end of the line, He eventually came to Judea and to Jerusalem where He would be crucified. His visit to planet Earth would indeed be a hostile one.

Yet that first peaceful night, when the angels of heaven told the shepherds of His soft, soft landing, it was just the beginning. Just as Neil Armstrong planted the American flag on the moon's surface declaring the beginning of space exploration, so too the Saviour planted His flag on planet Earth, declaring He would one day redeem it in His own time. And His banner over us was love.

> One tiny step is all He took
> but O the gulf He spanned!
> For us He donned those peasant rags
> and left Immanuel's Land.

December 1

"Thanks be unto God for his unspeakable gift."
2 Corinthians 9:15

Some Bible translations relate His gift as *"indescribable."* Some translators prefer the word, *"unspeakable."* It is all the same to me. To me, the gift of Christ is both indescribably wonderful and unspeakably profound. Words only fail when we attempt to describe Him entirely. Like the Jews of old, who did not dare pronounce the sacred name of God, or even spell it, so too we should feel there is something unspeakable about that name—something to muzzle us into silent wonder. The song writers have discovered it, penning the words "Jesus, Jesus, Jesus, there's just something about that name" (*There's Something About That Name*, Bill & Gloria Gaither). A more modern version puts it this way: "Will I stand in Your presence or to my knees will I fall? Will I sing for You, Jesus? Will I be able to speak at all? I can only imagine, I can only imagine" (*I Can Only Imagine*, MercyMe).

Even humanly speaking, the gift of a child or spouse is practically unlimited. My wife is an endless source of encouragement, comfort and grace to me. Each day, each week, each month, and each year she brings me new blessings, not to mention the blessing she has been to me all these years. The children provide almost limitless enjoyment, too. Each new day they tickle my heart with joy and laughter. Each phase of their lives brings me fulfillment, satisfaction and purpose as I see them mature, reaching the different milestones of life.

If we find the gifts of children and spouses extremely fulfilling, how much more the Giver and Creator of those blessings! The day we were saved, that moment when we first trusted in Christ as Saviour, was the moment we undid the bow and ribbon of that illimitable gift. Speaking of that gift, the Apostle John wrote in the prologue to his gospel, *"And of his fulness have all we received, and grace for grace"* (John 1:16).

Who can tell how many countless times He has blessed us? Who can tell how many times He has restrained Himself from giving us what we justly deserve? Jesus Christ is the everlasting well from whom we draw cup after cup of blessing, the treasure house in which we find gift upon gift of grace, and the storehouse from which we receive load upon load of goodness. I agree with the Psalmist who every morning must have awakened and shouted, *"Blessed be the Lord, Who daily loads us with benefits, The God of our salvation!"* (Ps. 68:19, NKJV).

And what were the benefits he was shouting about? Creation was the first gift, then followed His gifts of Sustainer, Illuminator, Teacher and Saviour. But that's not all. Now He is Redeemer, Intercessor, Shepherd, Provider and our Great High Priest, who constantly tends and ministers to us in our times of need. But that's not all. In a coming day, He will crown us more with the gifts of Husband, King and Glorifier of His people. What else can be said but thanks be to God for His immeasurable, incalculable, incomparable gift!

> On that first Christmas night
> silently the tiny gift
> descended
> into the manger
> beneath the shadow of the Tree.

 December 2

"...a body hast thou prepared me."
Hebrews 10:5

A number of years ago I stood looking at a piece of abstract art by Picasso. I was impressed with the emotion it evoked in me and the message it contained about the horrors of war. But my sons thought it strange that I would stare so long at a piece of "junk" and couldn't understand why I was so intrigued by it. They were extremely bored and pulled at my sleeve to go.

So it is with Christmas for some people. They fail to see the wonder of it all, or rather they don't have the eyes to see. They don't realize the Artist of all creation has painted Himself into the landscape. They don't comprehend that the Sculptor of the human body gave Himself a body of His own and laid Himself in a manger. They fail to recognize that the Weaver of all plots weaved Himself into the very climax of the story. They yawn and move on, bored with the story they've heard all their lives.

But for those who can see it, Christmas is full of awe. Combining the omnipotent strength of the Almighty with the helpless whimper of an infant babe God became a man. This is the mystery of all mysteries. Never before had infinite deity become interwoven with perfect humanity. The genius of the Godhead saved His best performance till last: the Word was made flesh. The intricate tapestry of Christ's humanity and divinity had been hung up in Bethlehem and spread out in Galilee for all to see. In all those variegated colours of His earthly life we see all the marvels of His meekness, authority and wisdom.

In Him we see meekness and authority combined. With authority we see the high and lofty One denouncing the Pharisees and Sadducees for their hypocrisy. With meekness we see Him patiently investigating how long the boy with convulsions had had his illness (Mark 9:21). We see the infinitely wise One answering the Pharisees' and Sadducees' riddles by catching them in their own trapping questions. Yet we see the same infinitely wise One learning, asking and answering questions in the Temple (Luke 2:46).

Let us not think of the Incarnate God as a hybrid of humanity and divinity. The God-Man is not some sort of divine Minotaur, half human and half divine. He is fully God and yet, at the same time, fully man. Incomprehensibly, the Infinite One at Bethlehem became finite. Paradoxically, He was all powerful yet without strength as a babe. He knows all things yet has to learn everything. He is everywhere yet confined to Bethlehem's stable. Behold the mystery of the God-Man! There never has been anyone or anything on earth like Him before or since.

> Under the microscope we see
> the work of Bethlehem.
> For there we see Him split the cells
> and form the Son of Man.

December 2

"For in him dwelleth all the fulness of the Godhead bodily."   Colossians 2:9

A poem by George Herbert (1633) entitled *"Ungratefulness"* imagines the Incarnation and the Trinity as two cabinets which God has unlocked for all to see. He confesses that the Trinity is the "statelier" of the two, but admits that much of that cabinet is still locked. It will ultimately take death to fully unlock that cabinet, and even then we may not fully comprehend Him. Till then, we wait with anticipation to see Him unveiled, more of His fullness see.

Until then, the other cabinet, the Incarnation, has been thrown wide open for all mankind to see. To us belong the wonders of the mystery of God incarnate, Jesus of Nazareth. We have been invited, as it were, to enter into the stable, to gather around the manger, to peer in holy wonder and awe at the marvel of what God became in order to save us. This is the Lord's doing and it is marvellous in our eyes. It all started one quiet night somewhere in the soft rolling hills of one of the little towns of Judah, in Bethlehem Ephratha.

The Incarnation serves to amplify the attributes of God that were already revealed in the Old Testament. In fact, in the Old Testament we only see His "back parts" when compared with the fully revealed face of Jesus Christ in the New Testament. For example, in Exodus 3:7 we hear the Almighty saying *"I know their sorrows."* But in the New Testament, in a much fuller, richer, tangible way we read that the Lord Almighty became an actual "Man of Sorrows" and was well acquainted with grief.

In this way, the Incarnation shows the character of God with greater magnification than ever before. If God's revelation in the Old Testament was at 4x magnification, then God's revelation in the New Testament would be at 40x magnification in comparison. And what will it be in heaven when "[we] *shall see his face*" (Rev. 22:4). His magnification will be past 400x! The best is yet to come!

Likewise, we see a greater amplification of His humility, or rather a further diminution of Himself. In the Old Testament we discover it is a humbling act for Him just *"to behold the things that are in heaven, and in the earth"* (Ps. 113:6) let alone to live among men, put up with them, and be treated with indignity. If it was humbling for Him just to look upon the things of the earth, how much more humbling was it to be born in a manger of all places?

White and blinding is the light
Where God in unapproachable light abides
But through the prism of His flesh
that Light has reached our eyes.

December 3

"But when the fulness of the time was come, God sent forth his Son, made of a woman, made under the law." Galatians 4:4

In the fullness of time God sent forth His Son into the world. That first Christmas was the precise moment when fullness of time had arrived, the initiation of God's ultimate rescue mission. Before the foundation of the world, before ever the clock of time began, before God ever gave the gift of freewill to mankind, God laid a safety net down. The Lamb was slain before the foundation of the world. Long before He was ever born, the Christ had already died. Before even a brick was laid, while the whole earth lay shrouded in darkness (Gen. 1:2), the Lord Jesus Christ lay at the bottom of the foundation, crucified, slain.

God started the world with a crucified Son. If somehow, by a magic crystal ball, you knew all your children would turn out to be belligerent, disrespectful citizens; if you knew they would squander your love and provision; worse yet, if you knew they would deliberately take the things that belong to you, embezzle them, and rob you of what was rightfully yours, would you still give birth to them? Most wouldn't but God did. God knew that at least half of humanity would take the gift and reject the Giver, that some would use their free will to worship Him, while others would use it to worship themselves.

But God so loved the world He laid a safety net down. Before God even said, *"Let there be light"* (Gen. 1:3), He knew that He would cry out in the darkness, *"My God, my God, why hast thou forsaken me?"* (Matt. 27:46). We would be banished from the paradise of God but the Son of God would serve our exile. All the prodigals who have sinned against Him can come home because He has slain the fatted calf. God Himself has paid the fare. Our bail has been paid, the sentence has been served, our paradise has been regained, and we are free. The Lord hung alone on the cold hard cross so that we would be seated at the long warm table of the consummate Christmas feast.

When the time was right God sent His Son into the world. As you go about making all your various preparations for the Christmas season, think of all the preparations God made in order to prepare for that very first Christmas. The descendants of Abraham were chosen, the tribe of Judah was selected, the dynasty of David was designated, and the peasant family of Mary and Joseph was chosen. The eternal clock had reached the dawn of redemption. It was time for the Son of God to be born. The countdown to the crucifixion had begun. If the cross was to be the ultimate fulfillment of redemption, then the incarnation was the penultimate. The chessboard was set: God first became a pawn in order to be crowned king.

The Father now looks daily for the return of His prodigals. The Shepherd searches endlessly for His sheep. The Spirit sweeps the globe looking for His lost coins. Down through the counsels of eternity (Eph. 1:11), up through the ancient lineage of Abraham and David (Matt. 1:1) into the world of rebellious and sinful men, the Son of God came. The seed of the woman had travelled from womb to womb to womb, to finally arrive one silent holy night on the plains of Bethlehem, ready from the foundation of the world.

> Down from the heights of heaven's glory
> Far from the shore of Paradise
> Down from the royal mount He plummeted
> into the dingy, narrow stall.

December 3

"And so terrible was the sight, that Moses said, I exceedingly fear and quake." Hebrews 12:21

When God Almighty revealed to Moses the law on Mount Sinai, He told him to tell the people not to come near the mountain. Anyone who did was to be thrust through with a dart to die. Even if so much as a beast touched the mountain, it was to be stoned to death or shot through with an arrow. To add terror to panic, the whole mountain range was set ablaze while the piercing sound of a trumpet blared louder and louder echoing throughout the valley. An angry fist shook the mountain and caused the ground to quake. Thunder cracked and lightning flashed to complete the scene. A very thick cloud of smoke hid Moses from their sight.

But it was completely different on Bethlehem's plain. Silent was the night. The trumpet was at rest. The crickets chirped, the flies buzzed about. No thunder. No lightning. No fire. Instead of a dark cloud blocking all vision from sight there was a bright and shining star illuminating the place where the Holy One slept. Unlike Moses, the shepherds did not exceedingly tremble. There in the manger lay the most innocuous symbol of all the earth: a helpless babe. The Lord of Hosts had become the child of Mary. Temporarily, God had hung up His bow. The root had sprung out of dry ground. For the time being, God had sheathed His flaming sword. Gone was the fire, and mild was the night. All was calm, all was bright. Yon young virgin, mother and child, sat silent in the manger stall. God had come to us, and had brought peace with Him.

When C. S. Lewis wrote *The Chronicles of Narnia*, he chose a lion as the image of Jesus Christ in order to portray both the ferocity and gentleness of God. Since nothing can be more ferocious than a lion, with its blood curdling roar and knife-like claws, Lewis chose it as his enduring symbol of Christ.

Yet nothing is more frolicsome and cuddlesome as a cat, so Lewis chose this image to reflect the pure goodness and awful severity of our God. Christ is both the Lion and the Lamb. God had transformed Himself into a harmless Child. To those who disobey He is like a ferocious lion. To those who reconcile with Him He is like a playful cat.

> The Lord, the ferocious lion,
> rips apart every cage
> that attempts to define Him,
> yet as a cub He came.

December 4

"He brought me up also out of an horrible pit, out of the miry clay..."   Psalm 40:2

On August 5, 2010, thirty-three miners lay trapped 2300 feet underground after a mineshaft collapsed in Northern Chile. All of Chile hoped and grieved for the men who were helplessly trapped below. On the surface of the earth, one hundred and thirty experts gathered to figure out a plan to rescue the men. The best plan they came up with was to dig a tunnel and send down a shuttle just big enough for one man. Each man would enter the shuttle and travel 15 minutes to the safety of the surface, out of that horrible pit, out of the miry clay. On that one long night, the shuttle was successful and all the miners were rescued.

We read in the New Testament of the Son of Man who *"descended first into the lower parts of the earth"* (Eph. 4:9). The Lord Jesus Christ is like that shuttle the miners used to escape their dungeon. By becoming flesh, He descended far down into the lowest parts of the earth, down from the heights of heaven into the dark chambers of men, down from being the centre of heaven's attention into the obscurity of Bethlehem's village where no place could be found for Him in the inn.

But down He came. He dove down in His incarnation and crucifixion in order that He might bring us up with Him in His resurrection and ascension. Just like the miners in Chile had no hope of ever rescuing themselves, we too were without hope in the world and could not by our own efforts rescue ourselves from the pit of God's judgment. But in the fullness of time, God sent His Son into the world to save us from the awful penalty of our sins. Forever we deserve to be confined under God's judgment in the pit of everlasting punishment where there will be weeping and gnashing of teeth. But praise God, Christ dove down into that glorious night.

Can you imagine the relief and elation the miners felt when that shuttle reached the bottom of the shaft? They would have felt just a taste of the eternal gratitude we feel toward our Lord Jesus Christ, who plunging down into the lowest parts of the earth pulled us up out of a horrible pit via the shuttle of His cross, into the safety of the empty tomb.

> He that descended
> is the same also that ascended
> up far above all heavens,
> that He might fill all things.

December 4

"...behold, there came wise men from the east to Jerusalem..."   Matthew 2:1

We all know the story. The wise men had seen His star in the East and had come to worship the One who was born King of the Jews. He who was the Light of the World picked the perfect symbol for His birth. A star heralded His arrival. It was no accident that the One who is "the Bright and Morning Star" was symbolized by a star. The star in the heavens lit the way, so to speak, so the wise men could find their way, just as Jesus would later say, *"As long as I am in the world, I am the light of the world"* (John 9:5).

It had been four hundred years since the prophet Malachi gave the last message that closed the Old Testament. It had been four hundred years of silence and darkness. Were there no more revelations from God? Yes, there was one more revelation, and the greatest revelation had been saved for last. Who could have foretold that the silence would be broken by an infant's gurgle? Who could have predicted that the darkness would be perforated by the tiny light of a child? Who knew that instead of a prophet, God would come Himself and speak His truth? These things boggle the mind and thrill the heart.

Most Sunday School Christmas skits portray the wise men as worshipping the Christ immediately after the shepherds depart, or concurrently with them. We know this is only "skitology," for in reality the wise men appeared months or even years later. Theirs was a long journey. When they finally found the infant Christ, He was in a house, not a manger. By that time, the shepherds were long gone. The reason the Scriptures present it this way is because Christ was sent first to the Jew—to those humble, lowly, Jewish shepherds—then to the Gentiles, those Magi from the East. This is God's way in the gospel. He gave it *"to the Jew first, and also to the Greek"* (Rom. 1:16).

In the coming of the Christ, none were excluded. The Christ came for all peoples of the earth, but He came to the Jews first in order to fulfill His promises to them, for God is a promise keeping God. Herod and the Jews rejected Him, but the Gentiles received Him and rejoiced with exceedingly great joy. Be filled with joy this Christmas and be a wise man still.

> Out of Jacob a star will arise
> And He shall bring healing in His wings,
> but first He dawned in Bethlehem
> A sparrow yet King of kings.

December 5

"And this shall be a sign unto you; Ye shall find the babe ..."   Luke 2:12

What did the shepherds find? They found an infant wrapped in swaddling clothes. They found a manger, some animals, and two peasant parents. That's it. No trumpets, no kings, no priests. That first Christmas was a quiet one for the One who had heard heaven's praises days after eternal day. But our God is a God who sometimes works with a still small voice.

What did they find? What they did not find was a pillar of cloud enveloping the plains of Bethlehem. What they did not find was a pillar of fire lighting up the path to where the Christ slept. Finally, He who was the glory of the Temple had arrived, but not a ray of outward glory shone in the stable that night. Nor did they find a pillar of fire lighting up the way to where the Child slept. Under His feet was not found *"a paved work of a sapphire stone"* (Ex. 24:10) but only hay, straw and perhaps animal dung. Stranger still, they did not find that *"the glory of the LORD"* had descended to fill the stable, as they did when they completed the tabernacle of His presence (Ex. 40:35). Everything looked strangely...normal. The ark had been covered with badger skins. There was no beauty that we should desire Him.

They neither heard nor saw the four living creatures gathered round the manger crying *"Holy, holy, holy"* (Rev. 4:8). Seraphs did not flit to and fro with wings covering their faces and feet. A whirlwind did not blow over the fields, nor did the Earth quake. No thunder. No flashes of lightning. Just an occasional gurgle from the mouth of the baby.

There were no visions of wheels within wheels, as Ezekiel saw (Ezek. 1:4-11). No rainbow encircled the manger like a throne, as John saw (Rev. 4:3). The smoke of incense did not fill the stable. On this occasion, Moses and Elijah remained in their graves and were not called upon to stand beside the manger. Only Joseph and Mary were present.

The birth of the Lord Jesus Christ is one of the reasons I strongly believe the Bible. The account of the greatest birth in history is told in such simple, uneventful terms, and with such economy that it must be viewed as either poor fiction or profound truth. If I were the author of the story there would be more detail, more action, and certainly more flourish for such a monumental occasion. But less is more. And the fact is, the Lord Jesus Christ certainly became less when He entered that manger, though by becoming something relatively less He became something infinitely more.

So what did the shepherds find? They found God, holy, harmless, undefiled, lying in a manger in need of swaddling clothes. They found a God of love who had come to save His people from their sins. They found the Lord of glory in a humble house of clay.

> For us He chose the manger
> For us He entered the stall
> For us He climbed Mount Calvary
> For me He gave His all.

December 5

"Therefore the Lord himself shall give you a sign; Behold, a virgin shall conceive, and bear a son, and shall call his name Immanuel." Isaiah 7:14

At a time when the world empire of Assyria was bulldozing the nations, Isaiah boldly proclaimed this prophecy of the victorious virgin child. While Tiglath-Pileser was busy amassing soldiers and horses and chariots, God was quietly planting a kingdom of His own. This gentle kingdom, as opposed to the cruel kingdom of the Assyrians, would be characterized by a Child, a virgin's Child, *"and the government shall be upon his shoulder: and...of the increase of his government and peace there shall be no end"* (Isa. 9:6-7).

I find it deliciously ironic and accurately prophetic that Isaiah announced his prophecy at the exact moment the Assyrian nation was on the rise. At a time when the King of Assyria thought he was the master of the chessboard, little did he know that God was using him as a pawn to ultimately bring in the kingdom of His Son. Isaiah predicted the overthrow of Assyria would come on the shoulders of a young child. Just as Syria and Israel would be conquered in no less than 65 years (Isa. 7:8) as a punishment for oppressing God's people, so too Assyria and every other nation of the earth would and will be smashed to pieces by the eternal kingdom of Christ. The prophecy of Immanuel signaled the beginning of the end.

They say it only takes a tiny crack in a massive edifice to bring the whole structure down. So it is with God and the kingdoms of this world. The fulfillment of Isaiah's prophecy 700 years later brought about a tiny crack in the kingdoms of men, the birth of the ultimate Immanuel. But it was from this tiny crack God made His entry into the world. From there the crack became a fissure and that fissure became a fault line, and one day the whole earth will be turned inside out through that first Christmas morn in Bethlehem Judea.

I love the chime of bells at Christmas time. One of the largest bells ever fashioned by the hands of men resides in Notre Dame, France. So huge is the bell that its tongue alone weighs 500 lbs. On Christmas day its chime can be heard ringing throughout the streets of Notre Dame. They appropriately named that bell Emmanuel. In a similar way, I believe the birth of the Saviour has rung out all around the world. It started ringing in Bethlehem first, then Galilee, then Judea, then Samaria, then to the uttermost parts of the earth. "Joy to the world the Saviour reigns" (*Joy to the World*, Isaac Watts).

When first chimed that tiny bell,
Not many heard the sound,
But when the virgin's child is found
He'll smash the gates of hell.

December 6

"In whom are hid all the treasures..."
Colossians 2:3

Out of the gift of Christmas comes every other gift. Remember when you were a kid and someone had the not-so-novel idea to wrap a big gift, which, when it was opened, had another wrapped gift inside, then another, then another? The gift of salvation is like that. In Him are gifts of sanctification, adoption, justification, glorification, redemption, wisdom and grace upon grace. In Christ are hidden all the treasures of life and godliness. If you have Him, you have peace. If you have Him, you have strength to do the will of God. If you have Him, you have comfort in all your afflictions. With Him you have everything. The manger contained the gift that contained everything else.

Christmas is sort of like a reverse Pandora's Box. When Pandora opened the forbidden box, every evil and foul thing came out of it and plunged the world into despair. But when God opened Mary's womb to give us the Christ, every good and perfect gift came with Him and blessed the world with everlasting consolation.

The manger is like a treasure chest as well, which upon discovery yields precious and endless treasure. In Christ we keep discovering and receiving grace. The Magi from the East were the first of many to follow their treasure map in the stars and discover the riches of Christ. Many have followed the treasure map of His Word since and have found Him there.

His gifts are not cheap either, like silver or gold which corrupts with time, but rather are eternal and soul-enriching. Grace and peace are a part of the daily treasure He grants us in which to revel. Mercy and hope are other rubies of His collection, not to mention wisdom and knowledge and truth. All of it is ours in Christ. *"...all things are yours"* declared the Apostle Paul to the undeserving Corinthians, *"...the world, or life, or death, or things present, or things to come; all are yours"* (1 Cor. 3:21-22).

A passport gives you access to a foreign country and allows you to enjoy all its attractions. Christ is the passport into God's kingdom, without which we will never enter or see the kingdom of God. Receiving Him gives us access to His riches and grace. And great are the riches of Immanuel's land. Pleasant delights and rivers of pleasure are found there (Ps. 36:8). Liberally He gives His wisdom to us, and full of goodness is His sack—far greater than any imaginary Santa Claus at the North Pole.

Let us rediscover the riches of Bethlehem's treasure again this Christmas season.

In Him, Jew and Gentile come together
In Him, East and West reclaim their centre
In Him, the brokenhearted find their mender
In Him, mercy and truth deeply kiss.

December 6

*"...yea, though we have known Christ after the flesh,
yet now henceforth know we him no more."*

2 Corinthians 5:16

In "The Dwarf Trees," a Japanese Noh play written in the fourteenth or fifteenth century, an Emperor disguises himself as a wandering priest in order to learn something of his subjects. On a cold, snowy night he stood outside a village home to see if anyone would give him lodging. At first an old couple turned him away, thinking he was just a peasant priest, but afterwards they thought better of it and offered him some hospitality. Being poor themselves, they didn't have much, but what they did have they offered to him. After a humble meal, a warm fire and a good night's sleep, the Emperor-disguised-as-priest bid them farewell, and returned to his palace.

Did not the same event take place that first night in Bethlehem? The Son of God, awesome, majestic, dwelling in light unapproachable, came to us disguised as a mere human child, clothed in weakness and humility. To describe what happened, using majestic language, I will borrow a phrase from John Milton's poem on the nativity: "that glorious form, that insufferable light, that far-beaming blaze of majesty, He laid aside...and chose to dwell with us in a darksome house of clay" (*On the Morning of Christ's Nativity*, John Milton). The sun of the whole redemptive universe was made a flickering candle to extinguish the darkness of the world.

Though He has been inducted millions of times into the hall of fame in heaven, He made Himself of no reputation here on planet Earth in order to meet our greatest need. He who is the firstborn of all creation let Himself be tossed and jostled about in the streets of Nazareth as a nobody. The theme of angels' songs became the ragtime tune of the drunkards (Ps. 69:12). His reproach was worse than Job's though His net worth would bankrupt heaven if He ever withdrew.

But not everyone treated Him with indignity that night. Someone owned that stable and offered his parents whatever hospitality they could. A few shepherds did receive His birth announcement with rejoicing, and would not sleep till they had set their eyes on the Christ, wrapped in swaddling clothes and lying in a manger, just as the angels said.

Indeed the Emperor of the earth had come, not merely disguised as an infant but as an infant in truth. He came to give Himself up as an offering for sin. He came to reveal the length and depth and height of His love. Disguising Himself, He revealed Himself. He revealed His heart, and proved what lengths He would go in order to seek and to save that which was lost. O praise His Name forever, Christ the Lord.

> The King of glory masked His face
> and told us "Do not fear,"
> Extinguished that consuming fire
> to bid us to draw near.

December 7

"And this shall be a sign unto you; Ye shall find the babe wrapped in swaddling clothes, lying in a manger." Luke 2:12

Moses was also a shepherd who watched his flocks by night. To him God appeared in a burning bush to reveal His great plan to rescue Israel from their oppression in Egypt. God revealed Himself in glorious mystery through the burning bush and there displayed His might by turning a stick into a snake and a clean hand into a leprous one, then healed it, making it clean again. O what a glorious sight that must have been!

But what did the shepherds see when God spoke to them that first Christmas night? Did they see an inexhaustible flaming bush like Moses saw, speaking to them about the awesome rescue plan God was about to unfold? No, they saw a simple infant wrapped surrounded by hay, lying in a manger. To deliver Israel from Egypt required a display of God's raw, earth shaking power, but to deliver Israel from theirs sins it would take something more: a display of God's humiliation, dishonour and "defeat."

Did the shepherds see a stick turn into a snake, a clean hand-made leprous or water turned into blood? No, they saw something far greater. They saw the Invisible One made visible. They saw the Almighty One made weak. Marvel of marvels, they saw the Holy One and did not die. God had come near to us, and had allowed us to come near to Him. If this is a marvel to us, how much more marvellous is the fact that the Holy One, whom the heaven of heavens cannot contain, dwells not in a manger, but in the filthy stalls of our own hearts. God in me is a much greater paradox than God with us.

Charles Wesley's hymn has always captured the nature of the incarnation for me: "Veiled in flesh the Godhead see, hail the incarnate deity, pleased as man with men to dwell,

Jesus our Immanuel" (*Hark! The Herald Angels Sing*, Charles Wesley). In the soft sinews of the incarnation the Divinity had interwoven Himself with our humanity. The hand that would forever hold the scepter of the Earth would be a human-divine one permanently.

But what did the shepherds see? They saw the most precious ruby of the world wrapped in the simplest of all cloths. They found the greatest of treasure of the whole earth buried somewhere in the back fields of Bethlehem. They beheld the sweetest, cleanest, gentlest lamb they had ever had the privilege of seeing moments after its birth. O what a glorious sight!

> Into the tree of Adam's race
> Our Lord was grafted in,
> A man, yet not a man like us,
> A true branch without sin.

December 7

> *"...they shall call his name Emmanuel, which being interpreted is, God with us."* Matthew 1:23

When something is too complicated or too foreign to our understanding, when we don't have the capacity to grasp a new or difficult concept, it must be translated for us in terms that we know so that we can understand. The Incarnation provided that translation for us. God, whose greatness is unsearchable, whose character is infinite, whose face is inscrutable, came down in human form that we might see the invisible attributes of God in the Man Christ Jesus.

That is what John meant when he wrote, *"And the Word was made flesh, and dwelt among us, (and we beheld his glory...)"* (John 1:14). Because the sun was blindingly brilliant and because we do not have the capacity to comprehend the fullness of its light, God made Himself of a lesser wattage that we might better see Him. In this way, the Incarnation both veiled and unveiled the glory of God so that we could better understand what He is like.

"No one has seen God at any time" (John 1:18, NKJV). John wrote at the end of his introduction, summing up the revelation of God's mysterious nature as revealed to us in the Old Testament. But John continues and says, *"The only begotten Son, who is in the bosom of the Father, He has declared Him."* (John 1:18, NKJV). That is to say, He has interpreted Him. God pulled back the curtain and has displayed Himself to us. The Christ is the perfect explanation of God to us in plain clothes. This is the glory and meaning of Christmas, that God would dim Himself in order to enlighten our minds.

In 1799 French soldiers discovered an artifact that unlocked the hitherto unknown language of Egyptian hieroglyphics. Written in 196 BC, the ancient stele contained a script written in three languages or dialects: Greek, Demotic and Egyptian. It was through a working knowledge of the Greek language that the Egyptian hieroglyphs on the stele could be interpreted. To us, the Incarnation works in the same way. Christ is the Rosetta Stone who interprets God. Through Him we understand what God is like. In Him we see the tenderness of His nature. In Him we see the intensity of His love. In Him we see the fullness of His wisdom. In fact, in Him we see everything. He is the perfect revelation of God, so far as earthly eyes will ever see.

The writing of the Rosetta Stone in 196 BC gave us an understanding of Egyptian hieroglyphics, but praise God, the writing of the Godhead into human flesh gave us a deeper, richer and fuller understanding of His character, holiness and love, translated to us though the face of Christ.

<blockquote>
God's no longer a mystery
For Christ has made Him known.
For God has lived in history,
A body was His home.
</blockquote>

 December 8

"...And he went down with them, and came to Nazareth, and was subject unto them..."
Luke 2:51

The body is a powerful communicator. By its very presence it communicates. Never being home, many fathers have communicated to their families that other things are obviously more important than being home. On the other hand, many mothers have communicated to their children just how special they are by simply being there when they wake up in the morning, come home from school, or are being tucked into their beds at night. Parents who make the effort to be in attendance at as many of their children's sports games, recitals or performances indirectly, but directly, communicate they feel their children are worth investing in.

In the same way, God's bodily presence on this earth communicates His love. When He appeared over two thousand years ago, He demonstrated that He loved us. He came seeking that which was lost. He stood calling out our names on the streets. The cross proved there was nothing He wouldn't do to redeem us from our wicked ways. He obviously felt it was worth being here. By living here for thirty-three years, and dying **there** for three dark apocalyptic hours, He displayed His great love for all to see. All this He did to illustrate that little word *"so."* *"For God so loved the world, that he gave his only begotten Son, that whosoever believeth in him should not perish, but have everlasting life"* (John 3:16).

Perhaps an illustration will help. It is a well-known fact that Nelson Mandela spent 27 years in prison as a political prisoner, most of which was spent on Robben Island where he was known only as prisoner #46664. When tourists see the size of the prison cell he sat in for almost thirty years, when they look out the window he must have peered through, when they see the mirror in which he must have watched his hair turn gray, their hearts are melted with empathy. To the people of South Africa, Nelson Mandela has provided proof of his love for them and their nation. With his body he suffered so that South Africans could be free from hate and disunity. Mandela's imprisonment and suffering quietly qualified him for his term of presidency and communicated better than anything else his commitment to his people.

The writer to the Hebrews wrote that the Captain and Author of our salvation *"He learned obedience by the things which He suffered"* (Heb. 5:8, NKJV). That doesn't mean it was possible for Him to disobey. That doesn't mean He could have sinned. What it means is He learned obedience by the things which He suffered, things such as fatigue, bereavement, weariness, betrayal, etc., in order that He might sympathize with the ones He would be leading. That's what it means, and that's a wonderful truth. The Son of God suffered that you might feel His sympathy in your suffering.

Since we suffer on this earth, He suffered along with us. By suffering He became perfectly qualified to be our Great High Priest, having been *"taken from among men"* (Heb. 5:1), and made *"subject to weakness"* (Heb. 5:2, NKJV) in order that He might sympathize with us. For us He lived within the confines of a small house in Nazareth. For us He looked out the window of his father's carpenter shop for thirty years. For us He walked the narrow streets of Galilee.

> Thus God was made a licensed priest
> Of weakness and of woe,
> born into pain and reared in grief
> to echo with our souls.

December 8

"...and he shall reign for ever and ever."
Revelation 11:15

It has become a tradition to stand up during the Hallelujah chorus at the end of Handel's Messiah. And why shouldn't we? By standing we are paying tribute to the most important accomplishment in all history, human or angelic. By standing we are giving honour to the greatest King in all heaven and earth. By standing, and singing "Hallelujah," we acknowledge God is worthy of all adoration, praise, and glory.

We stand when we are in the presence of something great or in the presence of someone of great importance. In our schools, we stand every day for the singing of our national anthem, paying tribute to the freedom and greatness of our respective homelands. At weddings, we rise upon the entry of the one who is the centre of the whole occasion—the bride. At funerals, we rise to honour the body of the deceased and pay our respect to the sanctity of human life. How much more we should rise to give honour and blessing and glory to the King of kings and Lord of lords, who humbled Himself to become *"the Servant of rulers"* and the One *"whom man despises"* (Isa. 49:7, NKJV). *"O for a thousand tongues to sing my great Redeemer's praise"* (*O For a Thousand Tongues to Sing*, Charles Wesley).

I can think of at least three triumphant reasons to stand and give Him my "Hallelujahs." Firstly, He deserves a "Hallelujah" for descending into Mary's womb. The infinite expansive One shrank Himself into a cell no bigger than a nanometer. He did this, retaining all the attributes of His divinity while adding a pure form of humanity to Himself for the first time ever in His divine essence. From Mount Everest heights of heavenly glory our Saviour descended into the cold, dark caverns of the sons of men. In a sense, He demoted Himself to live in the womb of a woman of planet Earth, though by demoting Himself He promoted Himself even further in glory and rank. When Mary had given birth, His humiliation continued. The Lord dwelt for thirty-three years in the trenches of planet Earth, trenches far darker and lower than even Marianas Trench, and far more horrifying to His holiness than the atrocities experienced by the soldiers of WWI.

He deserves another "Hallelujah" for the humble way He lived. Though He deserved to be *"Enthroned in the praises of Israel"* (Ps. 22:3, NKJV), He endured the accusations and insults made upon His majesty. They called Him a liar. They called Him a fool. They called Him a devil. The One who is the greatest celebrity of heaven grew up a relative stranger on the streets of Nazareth, and at the end of His life they mistook Him as just another enemy of the Roman Empire, worthy of death by a cross. Though He was the Desire of all Nations, *"there is no beauty that we should desire him"* (Isa. 53:2).

Lastly, He deserves a final resounding "Hallelujah" for the cross He humbly died on. Could you do it? Could you bear the sins of the world and be punished for them? Then give Him your "Hallelujah" for doing it for you. For all eternity heaven will echo that last and final Hallelujah. Holy, Holy, Holy is the Lord Almighty because He died, died, died for me. I will gladly stand for the singing of our Saviour's international anthem, both now and in eternity.

> Hallelujah! the manger announced,
> Hallelujah! the tree proclaimed,
> Hallelujah! the tomb now echoes,
> Hallelujah, Hallelujah, Hallelujah He saves!

December 9

> *"...though your sins be as scarlet, they shall be as white as snow..."*   Isaiah 1:18

I don't care much for the cold and chill of winter, but I do appreciate its beauty. The bridal dressed trees remind me of the purity of Christ's righteousness. When the moonlight caresses the evening and my breath spumes a silver stream in the perfect stillness, the peace of a late December night reminds me that I am redeemed and all is well with my soul. The white flannel quilt thrown over everything in the morning tells me I am covered in Christ's righteousness. Gently falling flakes speak to me of the softly descended Spirit, the Dove of God upon my life.

To me, the snow covered earth looks most beautiful in the early dawn. Some unheard music caused by the sun glinting off the top of the snow causes thousands of shimmering diamonds to dance in unison. I squint and devour the beauty. Something in me loves the slight muscle strain I feel behind my eyes as I stare out the window, completely mesmerized. I put the coffee on, I read my Bible, I celebrate the season.

But then something forbidden happens. The plow lumbers up the street. The scraping of windows, the shovelling of sidewalks, the churning of engines begin to muzzle the silence. The motors chug and churn in their driveways spitting up bile and blackness from their mufflers. Black tires leave tread marks like scars on the street. People file out of their homes with no time to appreciate the wonder of it all. In less than an hour they have trampled the beauty of the snow. What took God an evening's worth of artistic effort was destroyed by men in an hour.

But to me, the true beauty still remains. The picture of the morning snowfall serves as a reminder of things eternal. Nothing can touch the snow-white righteousness of Christ which He sent down for us that first Christmas night. The hustle and bustle of men cannot disturb it. No tool of man can desecrate the work that has been done.

I am so glad Christ came. I am so thankful He descended on the plains of Bethlehem like snow one Christmas night long ago. Though I am stained with sin, He has bleached me whiter than snow. Though I am blackened with soot, like the grey mush on the side of the street, yet He looks upon me as pure as the freshly fallen snow of the morning—covered in a righteousness that can never melt away. Praise God for the gift of Bethlehem and Calvary. Bless God for the gift of the Christ.

> White, pure white is the silent flake
> Dark, dark red, the blood of Christ.
> But His stain can make the putrid pure
> His blood can bleach the foul white.

December 9

"That which was from the beginning, which we have heard, which we have seen with our eyes, which we have looked upon, and our hands have handled..."
1 John 1:1

The men of Beth Shemesh would have been shocked to read this verse. We should be shocked too. In 1 Samuel chapter 6 we read that the Ark of the Covenant had been captured by the Philistines. Because the Ark would not abide in the same Temple as Dagon, the Philistine's god, and since the Philistines had been stricken with tumours because of it, the five lords of the Philistines decided to send it back to Israel in hopes that they might be healed.

The plan was to place the Ark on an oxcart led by two cows which had just given birth. They separated the calves from their mothers and let the cows pull the cart to see where they would go. As if drawn by an invisible hand, the cows abandoned their young and went straight up to the village in Israel called Beth Shemesh.

When the Ark arrived, the people of Beth Shemesh rejoiced. The Ark had returned! They immediately broke up the oxcart and sacrificed the cows as an offering. This was good. But what they did next was a grave error. They decided to remove the lid and peer inside the Ark. To do so was forbidden on pain of death. But the villagers persisted. Immediately a large number of them were struck dead. Those who remained cried out, *"Who is able to stand before this holy Lord God?"* (1 Sam. 6:20).

Fast forward three thousand years. The land is still Israel but the field is no longer Beth Shemesh. It is Bethlehem. The Ark of the Covenant, the symbol of God's presence, did not come to rest in the corner of a field, but the God of the Ark Himself. In a manger, not unlike that oxcart of old, the very God of the Ark rested, not in a chest of wood and gold, but in the sinews and bones and blood of an infant babe. Who is able to stand before this holy LORD God?

Nearby a group of shepherds kept watch over their flocks by night. It was these men whom the Lord invited to look "inside" the Ark, the little manger that held the Lord. This time He did not dwell between the cherubim but between the horses' heads. He was not surrounded by six-winged seraphim but with animals with cloven hooves which chewed the cud. What happened to them when they looked upon the Lord of glory? Did their eyes melt in their sockets? Did they fall victim to a plague? Did they fall down dead? No, they saw the God of Israel and lived!

What was the difference between the shepherds of Bethlehem and the villagers of Beth Shemesh? Was it because one group of men were reapers and the other shepherds? No, there was no difference between the men. The real difference was that for the first time in history God permitted men to see Him for the purpose of redemption. For the first time He allowed the hands of sinners to touch Him. For the purpose of revelation and salvation He made it possible for the ungodly to behold Him, handle Him and draw near to Him. This is the miracle of the Incarnation. This is the marvel of Christmas.

> To peer into the ark of God
> brought certain death to men
> but when they saw Him veiled in flesh
> It gave new life from heaven.

December 10

"And it was revealed unto him by the Holy Ghost, that he should not see death, before he had seen the Lord's Christ."   Luke 2:26

Simeon is sometimes forgotten in our Sunday School Christmas plays. But he was not forgotten by God. To him it was revealed that he would not see death before he had seen the Lord's Christ. If you are reading this book and do not know that Christ is your Saviour, then this would be my prayer for you: that you would not see death before you see the Lord's Christ, that you would not face death before you hold Him in your arms as yours. Hear the simple call of the gospel: *"everyone who sees the Son and believes in Him may have everlasting life"* (John 6:40, NKJV).

God became visible in order that we might see Him. The Word became flesh in order that we might better read Him. In fact, the holy, high and transcendent God came so near that many not only saw Him but touched and handled Him as well. Simeon was one of the first to see Him but there have been many more since. It does not matter if you are old or young, known or unknown, or from the North, South, East or West, God has come for you.

When speaking to children at Christmas time an illustration I often use is this: I place a small rectangular mirror in the bottom of a gift bag, and then I say to the kids, "I know what God wants for Christmas—it's here in this bag." I hold up the multi-coloured bag with the twine looped handles. With puzzled faces, the room falls silent and they stare at me. When their curiosity is at fever pitch, I begin to allow some of them to look into the bag. As each one sees themselves in the mirror in the bottom of the bag, they smile and I tell them that what they see is all God wants for Christmas. The biggest smile steals across their faces as each one begins to understand that God has come for us. God has come seeking that which was lost. He came seeking us in the person of Christ.

Simeon had lived a long life. When he was young, Israel was free from the hard yoke of Roman bondage. But in 40 BC Israel fell victim to Roman oppression. Simeon must have been a young man or a young boy at the time. Imagine how his heart must have longed for the Messiah to come. Picture how he must have prayed year after year to see the Saviour save his people. How happy he must have felt when it was revealed to him that he would not see death before he saw the Christ!

In the 21st century we long for the coming of Christ again. The Simeons among us are longing to see the Christ. We know that one day He will come. But which of us will be alive when it happens? Perhaps it will be this generation. Perhaps it will be the next. But one thing is certain: *"the Lord himself shall descend from heaven with a shout"* (1 Thess. 4:16) and some of us will still be alive to see it. It may even happen this coming Christmas. Wouldn't that be the best gift ever—to wake up, not around the tree, but around the golden throne? Even so, Come, Lord Jesus!

When earth gives birth to heaven,
When the last curtain is drawn aside,
The Lord shall blossom, flower and bloom.
and spring shall forever abide.

December 10

*"He has put down the mighty from their thrones,
And exalted the lowly."*   Luke 1:52, NKJV

They say, actions speak louder than words. If this is true, let us pay careful attention to the action of the Christmas story so that we may better understand its message.

First of all, it was to shepherds that God first announced the birth of His Son. Not to the chief priests, not to the Pharisees, and not to scribes—but to shepherds. Shepherds in first century Palestine were traditionally poor, uneducated and low on the social ladder. Some scholars have even discovered through Rabbinic traditions that shepherds were considered defiled and unclean. From what we know of the arrogance and holier-than-thou attitude of the religious leaders of the New Testament, this should not come as a surprise.

What is surprising is that God tramples on these cultural taboos by deliberately inviting the shepherds to visit the newborn Messiah. The shepherds' shock at such an astonishing announcement is to be assumed. But this should come as no shock to us. True to form, God practiced what He preached. Jesus taught us, *"When thou makest a dinner or a supper, call not thy friends, nor thy brethren, neither thy kinsmen, nor thy rich neighbours...But when thou makest a feast, call the poor, the maimed, the lame, the blind"* (Luke 14:12-13). The God who taught us to invite the poor showed us the way that first Christmas night. God invited the shepherds first, giving them the place of honour.

It is evident that God exalts the lowly. That is who God is. He resists the proud but gives grace to the humble (Jas. 4:6). If Jesus were to be born today, He would not invite the high rollers of Wall Street to come and see the birth. He would not invite the sheiks and sultans who live in ornate palaces. It would be the street vendors, the sweatshop workers, the rickshaw drivers and the day labourers who were first invited to come. He does this to put down the mighty. He does this to encourage, exalt and endear the lowly. He reveals Himself to babes and hides Himself from the wise and prudent (Matt. 11:25).

Not only is God's love inclusive of all mankind but so is His mission. He invites everyone to come and see His Son. He invites all who come to go out and tell others to come. The invitation is twofold: first, come and see; second, go and tell. He who would later use fishermen to turn the world upside down was not ashamed to use shepherds to do the job in the beginning. Today He uses you and me.

Are you small? Is your profession a simple or lowly one? Good, that's exactly what God specializes in.

> On top of the lone mountain
> Far from the palace and parade
> the flower coyly opened to the sky.

 # December 11

> *"So it was that the ark remained in Kirjath Jearim a long time; it was there twenty years."*
>
> 1 Samuel 7:1

It is no wonder God used the sinful womb of Mary to house His Son. It is no wonder God used the sinful fathering of Joseph to raise Him to adulthood. It is also no wonder God allowed His Son to grow up in a household of sinful sisters and four unbelieving brothers named James, Joses, Judas and Simon (Mark 6:3). Why? This was nothing new. God had allowed Himself to be treated in a similar way on a number of occasions in the Old Testament.

For twenty years the ark remained in Kirjath Jearim, marooned outside the sacred structure of the Tabernacle, outside the holy designated vicinity of Shiloh. Before that the ark, the very symbol of the Presence of God, resided for a few months in the demonic temple of Dagon, the abomination of the Philistines. But most shocking of all, the ark of the covenant continued to reside in the midst of a stubborn, rebellious and sin-laden people who served God with their lips but denied Him in their hearts.

God has had His share of experiences dwelling with sinful men. The whole globe is crawling with them. There is nowhere He can dwell among us that is not teeming with ungodly sinners. That is why God could descend into the sinful body of Mary. That is how the Holy One was able to dwell in the sinful home of Joseph. Since the beginning of time God has often sat at the table with sinners. Such is the patience of God.

Just as God resided in Kirjath Jearim for twenty years, away from the proper worship and adoration due His holy name, so too the Presence of Israel resided in the house of Joseph and Mary for thirty years, away from the proper worship due His name. For twenty silent years God resided in the village of Kirjath Jearim, though He did not belong there; and for thirty more years God spent time in Mary and Joseph's home, though He did not belong there.

The ark was made of acacia wood covered with pure gold. The ark is a picture of the Incarnation, the acacia wood representing His perfect humanity, the gold representing His perfect deity. God and man wedded into one. The dwelling of the Presence of God among them via the Ark of the Covenant was a foreshadowing of the time He would spend tabernacling here (John 1:14). The jostling of the ark, the indignity it suffered when touched by Uzzah's hand, and its temporary sheltering in places unworthy of His name painted a picture of what was to come. God would indeed dwell with man. But He didn't belong here anymore than a diamond belongs in a manure pile.

> Into a chest of rotting wood
> The living God came down,
> but in a womb, in human flesh
> God incorruptible was found.

December 11

"And he sat down, and called the twelve, and saith unto them, If any man desire to be first, the same shall be last of all, and servant of all." Mark 9:35

The towel, the cross and the manger all tell the same story. The Lord has set the bar low. His was the greatest act of humiliation the world had ever seen, for never before or since had One so high become so low. The One who said to His disciples, *"If any man desire to be first, the same shall be last of all"* (Mark 9:35), was born last of all. He set the example Himself by entering our world without pageantry, without fanfare, without notice. "Who is He in yonder stall?" (*Who is He in Yonder Stall*, Benjamin Russell Hanby) the occupants of the inn could have asked. It was the Lord of glory but no one knew it.

The birth of the Saviour characterized His life and mission. Since He was to be despised and rejected in His life, humble and ignored was His birth. When our Saviour unrobed Himself and took up a servant's apron to wash the disciples' feet in the upper room, He had already done so thirty years before. Coming from heaven, arrayed in glorious majesty, He divested Himself of all His outshining glory, *"took upon him the form of a servant, and was made in the likeness of men"* (Phil. 2:7). The swaddling clothes, the servant's apron, and the linen graveclothes tell the story and comprise the wardrobe of His humiliation.

And the cross only added insult to injury. At His birth He was treated as a stranger. In His life He was treated as a madman. But on the cross He was executed as a criminal. The "first of all" had become the "last of all." Our Lord lived out the sermons He preached, as a living illustration. From birth to death His was a life of self-denial, hardship, and lowly service. At His birth there was no room for Him at the inn; in His life there was no place for Him to lay His head. And only one friend, His mother, and a few other women were there at His death. He left the world the same way He entered it—with nothing.

Yet this is the One whom the heaven of heavens cannot contain! How did He even fit all of Himself into that tiny little manger? With heaven as His throne and earth as His footstool, how is it that He had nowhere to lay His head? How can it be that He to whom all heaven kneels, Himself knelt down and washed the disciples' feet? Most amazing of all, how was it that the holiest of all was numbered among the transgressors of the earth? There is only one explanation: *"This is the LORD's doing; it is marvellous in our eyes"* (Ps. 118:23).

> He who sat enthroned in praises,
> Enshrined in the Temple of God,
> Behold Him now in yonder stall,
> encircled by horses, goats, sheep and cows.

December 12

> *"And suddenly there was with the angel a multitude of the heavenly host..."*   Luke 2:13

We often say that no one took notice of Christ's humble birth. On earth this was true. Only Mary, Joseph and a few humble shepherds laid eyes on the newborn king. All others missed out on that first private viewing. Only a few were invited into the birthing room that night to see the Child. This is the earthly side of the birth of Christ.

But the heavenly side is different. In heaven, the birth announcement must have rung throughout the hills and valleys of Immanuel's Land. There the cherubim, the coverers of God's glory, gathered to see His glory shine in human flesh. There the seraphim hovering with two wings must have viewed the holy manger with covered faces and veiled feet. There, they who continually chant *"Holy, holy, holy"* (Isa. 6:3) broke their custom for the occasion to join the heavenly host, shouting *"Glory to God in the highest"* (Luke 2:14).

Just as birthday guests gather expectantly in the dark to yell, "Surprise!" at the precise moment the birthday boy or girl arrives, so the whole heavenly host had gathered in joyful expectation, waiting for their moment to yell to planet earth, *"Peace, good will toward men"* (Luke 2:14). First to ever experience the restless suspense of a Christmas Eve was the heavenly host as they anticipated that first holy night. The holy angels must have felt like children waiting for Christmas morning to begin.

When Prince William and Kate Middleton were expecting the arrival of their firstborn son in July 2013, it seemed like the whole world waited with them. All hearts anticipated the arrival of the new heir to the throne. The press continued to give updates and reports on the status and progress of the birth. Finally, the long awaited moment arrived: Prince

George Alexander Louis was born into the world. All England rejoiced. An heir to the throne of Great Britain was born.

The same was true of Christ. His arrival may have gone unnoticed on earth but in heaven there was great glory attending His arrival. The whole night sky lit up with fireworks, as it were, *"and the glory of the Lord shone round about them"* (Luke 2:9). *"Glory to God in the highest"* (Luke 2:14) reverberated throughout the heavens, which must have gone echoing down the golden street. The royal Son, the Heir of all things, had arrived. And all of heaven rejoiced.

Glory to God for Creation
And glory for the Flood,
But glory to God in the Highest
For sending us His precious Son.

December 12

*"And in the sixth month the angel Gabriel was sent
from God unto a city of Galilee, named Nazareth..."*
Luke 1:26

"O Lord, how can it be? To me have You granted the privilege of announcing the most pivotal event of all human history, the Incarnation of Your beloved Son? Will You indeed stoop to make Yourself a little lower than my fellow angels for the purpose of redeeming Your wayward creatures, this mankind? Have You granted to me, who am lower than the least of all the angels, the revelation of the mystery of Your Christ, O Lord, to make all men see what is the fellowship of the mystery, which from the beginning of the world has been hid in You, my blessed Lord? I praise You, O Lord, for making Your angels spirits and Your ministers a flame of fire sent forth to serve those who will inherit salvation—things angels desire to look into.

Long ago, O Lord, You sent me to Your servant Daniel to explain the meaning of the visions revealed to him, how the times of the Gentiles must reign until the coming of the Stone made without hands which from the heavens shall smash the kingdoms of men to usher in the kingdom of Your Christ, Your dear Son, whose name is blessed forever. To Daniel You sent me to give him skill to understand the meaning of that great vision of the seventy weeks determined for Your people, Israel, to make an end of sins, to make reconciliation for iniquity, to bring in everlasting righteousness, and finally, at last, to anoint the Most Holy.

But this Lord...this is different, this is monumental, this is like nothing You have ever done before. And can it be that I shall announce that my Lord shall descend from the cliff heights of His glory to descend into the lowest parts of the earth, that the High and Lofty One who inhabits eternity will indeed submit Himself to the clock-tick of time to enter the womb of a lowly peasant woman, the daughter of a fallen race of sinners who drink iniquity like water? What can I possibly say to explain to this frail creature that she has been chosen to incubate the omnipotent and unstoppable Seed from which all salvation shall flow, that her seed shall be planted, shall sprout and blossom and spread to cover the breadth of the whole earth, *'that at the name of Jesus every knee should bow, of things in heaven, and things in earth…'* (Phil. 2:10).

To do Your bidding, O Lord, I go. I shall tell this young mortal Your summons: *'Rejoice, highly favoured one, the Lord is with you; blessed are you among women!'"* (Luke 1:28, NKJV).

<blockquote>
O Gabriel, chief herald of the heavens
To you the gospel came first.
You were the stork sent down by the Dove
And from you we take the baton.
</blockquote>

December 13

"...Jesus was born in Bethlehem of Judaea in the days of Herod the king."   Matthew 2:1

There could not be a greater contrast: Herod the imposter king versus Jesus the true King of the Jews. To be born in the days of Herod in the first century was not a good time to be born. My friend pointed out that in order to truly appreciate the context of this verse and what it must have meant to the Jews who first heard it, we would need to change the name of Herod to Hitler. A modern version of the Christmas story could read, "Jesus was born in Poland in the days of Adolf Hitler, the Furor." This would give the original story its proper tone of tragedy.

Herod, in contrast to Christ, was not born king of the Jews. He jockeyed, schemed and killed in order to maintain his position. An Idumean by birth, a descendent of Edom, Herod was not Jewish and certainly was not a son of David. The Romans appointed Herod as ruler over Judea almost forty years prior to the birth of Christ, and over the years the old king had grown paranoid, egotistical and ruthless by the end.

History attests that Herod "the Great" was anything but great in the moral sense of the word. Yes, he may have been a great engineer and architect but he was also a brutal dictator. Scripture records how he killed all the male children of Bethlehem but that was only one of his atrocities. Among those whom Herod murdered, that we know of, were his uncle, his brother-in-law, three of his own sons, his mother-in-law, and one of his wives. In fact, anyone suspected of being a threat to his right to the throne of Israel was done away with—hence, the slaughter of Bethlehem's infants, just to make sure any rival claimant to the throne was no longer a menace.

But God's plans and purposes cannot be thwarted by mere men. A mosquito has a better chance of stopping a freight train than a sinner the promises of God. Rather it is God who frustrates the intentions of men, overturning their schemes, as it is written, *"The LORD bringeth the counsel of the heathen to nought: he maketh the devices of the people of none effect. The counsel of the LORD standeth for ever"* (Ps. 33:10-11).

Herod tried to kill the Christ when He was an infant. An angry mob of Nazarenes tried to throw Him off a cliff (Luke 4:29-30) but He walked right through them. Many times the Jews tried to stone Him. But every plot was foiled. Nothing could stop the feet of Christ from touching the foot of Mount Calvary. It was there He was to die. It was for this purpose He arrived in Bethlehem that night.

Endless chess moves ahead, the Lord
Who sees tomorrow as today
Moves the nations as He wills
since nothing His purpose can stay.

December 13

"And the angel said unto them, Fear not: for, behold, I bring you good tidings of great joy, which shall be to all people."   Luke 2:10

We have a lot of fun at Christmas time but it is not called "Funmas." We eat a lot of food at Christmas time and exchange gifts, but we do not call it "Eatmas" or "Giftmas." We visit with family, share our lives with one another and exchange sentiments of love to the people closest to us, but it is not to be regarded merely as "Familymas."

If there were no Christ in heaven, heaven would be no heaven at all. In the same way, if we allow Christ to be crowded out of Christmas, then Christmas is nothing but an empty shell. Christmas without Christ is like a story without a main character, a meal without food, a house with no people in it. If not sung from the heart, our Christmas carols must sound like nails on a chalkboard to Him. If an effort is not made to include and incorporate worship or prayer or reading the Bible into our Christmas season, then Christ has been left out. And yet it is His day!

Idols are those things which we allow to eclipse our worship and dedication to God. God gave us family and God gave us food, but when those things become the focus and main attraction of Christmas we have lost our way. The deception is subtle. What could be wrong with giving gifts to one another, with generosity and good cheer? Nothing is wrong with these things, so long as Christ is invited and sits in the centre seat of our Christmas celebrations. Let us remember our families but not at the expense of forgetting the Christ.

The Laodiceans were a church that had everything—or so it seemed. To those who visited their church they appeared rich, and looked as if they had need of nothing. But in reality, in God's eyes, they were *"wretched, and miserable, and poor, and blind, and naked"* (Rev. 3:17). The cheerful Christmas house can suffer the same problem as the Laodiceans. With delicious and aromatic foods the house can be filled. Large and numerous gifts can cluster the base of the tree. Faces familiar and precious can even people the house—yet all the while the Christmas Saviour may stand outside the door and knock, waiting to come in.

We must be deliberate at Christmas time. We must be intentional. Christ is not worshipped "just because" we give and receive gifts, eat food, visit and spend time together as families. After all, even the unbelievers do that. To us, Christmas must include more.

So let it be CHRIST-mas loud and clear. Do not let the season descend into merely "Giftmas." The Gift of all gifts should not be buried under the Christmas tree, nor eclipsed by the star on the tree. Rather let Him be the Star which crowns the top of all our celebrations.

Christ the feast, Christ the gift
Christ the song, Christ the carol
Christ the hearth, Christ the marrow.

 December 14

> *"Where is he that is born King of the Jews?"*
> Matthew 2:2

"We're all so tired. We've come such a long way. When we started out the land was locked in ice. Now the green of spring begins to push through. The star appeared in the East almost a year ago. It seems like such a long time since I saw my wife's beautiful face and heard my children's laughter. But the journey though long and difficult, will be worth it all when we see Christ.

We Magi have been studying the stars for centuries. I have been studying them my whole life. We are not kings — we are astrologers, and we hope to please our king with all our findings. Never in all our star gazing over the years have we observed such a phenomenon as this star.

With us we have carried gold, frankincense and myrrh to bestow at the foot of the Child. We assume these gifts will be considered nothing on account of all the other gifts that will be strewn about Him by His own countrymen. We only hope our gifts will be acceptable as well. We wonder, when we get there, if there will be any room to find lodgings. Perhaps we will not be permitted entrance into the city, on account of the many who will be gathered there.

We often stay up late talking by campfire. We dream of what it will be like when we see the Great King. In all the robes given to Him will there be one of our own Persian tapestries thrown about Him? In all the rubies cast at His feet, will there be some lapis lazuli, that gorgeous purple stone, native to our own region? In all the praises lavished on Him from those of His own countrymen, perhaps we will hear some praising Him in our own tongue? We stay up far too late talking about these things. In the morning we are reluctant to get out of our sacks and begin the journey again. But the star draws us onward.

We have heard legends and rumours of a great King Solomon who used to reign in that country. Of all the East he was reputed to be the greatest on account of his wisdom. We wonder if this king will be greater than he? King Solomon built a beautiful and majestic Temple, a marvel of architecture and engineering for his day, though it was destroyed by the tyrants of Babylon. We wonder, will the newborn king build a greater Temple than even King Solomon's?

Our minds swim with our thoughts as the camels plod on, by light of the sun by day, by light of the star by night. Soon we will arrive. We plan to go to Herod's palace first. Surely the tired old king has made great preparations for Him who is born King of the Jews. How could anyone fail to make preparations for the celebration of such a great king?"

> Praise shall be my frankincense
> Offerings my gold
> Myrrh shall be my holy walk
> As all my days unfold.

December 14

"...because there was no room for them in the inn."
Luke 2:7

Of course there are some who do not believe that Christ was born in a stable. Those who say such things are not necessarily atheists. They are theologians and scholars who feel the birth story of Christ has been misrepresented. They point out that the word "stable" is not even found in Luke 2. Due to an unfortunate translation, some scholars argue that there was no "inn" either. The Greek word for "inn" could also be translated as "room." In fact, in Luke's gospel, chapter 22, the same word for "inn" is used to describe the "upper room." In this interpretation of the story, Jesus was not born in a stable but in the house of a relative, most likely in the lower level where the animals were kept.

But to me the main message of the story remains the same. Whether He was born in a stable, in a cave, or in the basement of some relative's house, He was still among the beasts. Whether there was no room for Him in the inn or no room for Him in the house, the message remains the same: His was a humble birth. He was still born among the cows and the sheep. The dwelling did not smell of incense. It smelled of hay and urine and dung. Swaddling bands gave witness that He'd been emptied of His heavenly glory. The manger was the new Ark of His covenant. Peasants switch places with the cherubim and six-winged seraphim were replaced by the two-winged rooster.

I don't quibble about the details. I'm too much in awe of the main event. The Ancient of Days had become a child of time. He who was "of old" was now brand new. Our God who is a consuming fire was cold and needed swaddling. The Almighty for the first time ever was in need of something: human milk.

Israel marvelled at the supernatural strength of Samson. How could a human born child have such supernatural strength? But in Christ we find the opposite. Marvel that the One who is our Strength made Himself weak in order to save all those too weak to save themselves. Just as the Lord gave Samson supernatural strength to save Israel from her enemies, so too the Lord gave Himself supernatural weakness in order to save us from our sins.

What it took to save Israel in Samson's day was the death of the Philistines. But it took far more to save the world from sin. To save the world from sin it took the death of God's Son. In order for that to happen He was born in the city of David, whether it was in a stable or a cave, to taste death for everyone.

<blockquote>
A stable or a cave? No matter.
The main point: He came to save
Outside the inn or in a home?
His birth was still the humblest one.
</blockquote>

 December 15

"...we shall see him as he is..."   1 John 3:2

In the movie *Contact*, which I saw years ago, starring Jodie Foster, mankind discovers alien life in the universe. When the character Foster plays finally makes contact with the intelligent life forms who had been transmitting messages to planet Earth for centuries, they appear to her in human form. In fact, they appear to her in a very specific human form—they appear to her as her deceased father. The aliens chose to "meet" mankind for the first time in this way, because they thought it would be easier for mankind to understand. As it turns out, they were right. When Jodie Foster saw her father, she felt an immediate connection with the "Being" from another world.

Imagine what it would be like if God were to visit us in His totality. What if He came to us in total fullness, holding nothing back, raw and naked in His sublime essence? Would we be able to take it in? Or would our brains turn to mush? Even if we could somehow take it in, how would we even be able to communicate it?

John fainted when He saw only a vision of Him (Rev. 1:17). I imagine Isaiah curled up in the fetal position, when he saw Him and said, *"Woe is me! for I am undone...for mine eyes have seen the King, the Lord of hosts"* (Isa. 6:5). A vision of the Son of Man was revealed to Daniel, and he fell to the ground because *"I retained no strength"* (Dan. 10:8). These were the reactions of holy men who caught only a glimpse of Him. What will it be to see Him entirely, *"as he is"* (1 John 3:2)?

A mysterious fever struck Helen Keller when she was only nineteen months old, and for the rest of her life she remained deaf and blind. Unable to hear, unable to see, she did not understand the world of light and colour around her. But a dedicated teacher named Anne Sullivan committed her life to teaching Helen to "see." As a result, Helen learned to read, write and go on to earn a graduate degree from Harvard University. In the same way, Christ Jesus was our Anne Sullivan. Born spiritually deaf and blind because of sin, we could neither see God nor understand Him. That we might see, God clothed Himself in human flesh and walked among us.

"We shall see him as he is" (1 John 3:2), the Apostle John wrote, and we did see Him as He is when we saw Him in human flesh. But we did not see His totality. For that, we will have to wait till the end. New eyes are required to see that awesome sight. The first unveiling took place on Mount Sinai when God revealed Himself through words. To Moses it was revealed that the Lord is *"merciful and gracious, longsuffering, and abundant in goodness and truth"* (Ex. 34:6). The second unveiling occurred in Bethlehem when the merciful and gracious God invested Himself in human flesh. In Christ we beheld abundant mercy and abounding goodness.

But the third and final unveiling will occur when He returns to take His people home where His glory dwells, where we shall behold His glory. At that time we will finally *"see him as he is"* (1 John 3:2) and realize then that even in the gospel records *"the half was not told"* (1 Kgs. 10:7)!

As fire tries to warn the snow,
"You cannot see my face and live!"
So sinful minds just cannot know
The awesome holiness of God.

December 15

"And the Word was made flesh..." John 1:14

Just as a word communicates a thought, so Christ communicates God. Just as the word "dog" embodies all that a four-legged canine creature is, so the incarnate Christ embodies all that the invisible God is. Bethlehem's manger celebrates God's eternal explanation of Himself. *"...he that hath seen me hath seen the Father"* (John 14:9), Christ would later say. *"And we beheld his glory"* (John 1:14) was the Apostle John's summary of the whole event.

We read that God is good in the Old Testament. But in the New Testament we see Him doing good through the body of Jesus of Nazareth, who *"went about doing good"* (Acts 10:38). In the Old Testament we read that God possesses abundant mercy; in the New Testament we see Jesus healing the woman with the issue of blood, cleansing the ten lepers, stopping the funeral procession of the widow's son and raising him from the dead, giving sight to the blind and lifting the lame from the beggar's mat. In the Old Testament we find a record of God's mercy, but in the New Testament we get a whole parade of His merciful acts.

In Plato's *Republic,* an inquiry is made into the true nature of the just man. Almost four hundred years before Christ walked the earth, Plato imagined what the perfect man might look like. Among the many things Plato imagined, one of them was that the perfectly just man of necessity would need to be despised and regarded as unjust in order to prove that he wasn't practicing his righteousness as a means of gain. That is to say, His righteousness was not motivated by a desire to receive the praise of men. Only by being despised for their righteousness can truly just men prove their righteousness.

While Christ went about doing good men continued to ridicule and revile Him. When He arrived to raise Jairus' daughter from the dead, they laughed Him to scorn, thinking He could bring her back to life (Luke 8:53). In exchange for the good works He did, they attempted to stone Him. *"Many good works have I shewed you from my Father; for which of those works do ye stone me?"* (John 10:32).

Not only were His works good but His character was impeccable. He did no sin. He knew no sin. And in Him was no sin. Standing before His accusers and opponents, Christ was able to say with confidence, *"Which of you convinceth me of sin?"* (John 8:46).

What Plato envisaged, Christ literally became. Though Christ was completely righteous, yet He was regarded as a madman and a criminal. Not only did this prove that Christ was just, but it also proved that He was love. For us He made Himself of no reputation. For us He was regarded as a liar, a glutton, and an imposter. Yet in truth He was the One *"whose name is Holy"* (Isa. 57:15), though He did not demand men regard Him as such.

What Plato imagined in word, Christ actually became in flesh (and so much more). Had he lived at the time of Christ, Plato could say, *"And the Word was made flesh"* (John 1:14). The just man, a simple literary experiment for Plato, was an absolute necessity for the redemption of mankind. Christ died for our sins, *"the just for the unjust"* (1 Pet. 3:18), for without a perfectly just man, a sacrifice without spot or blemish, a substitute unsoiled by sin, we could never be saved.

Veiled in flesh, His glory tamed
He walked the streets of earth;
Unplugged, unheavened & unthroned
He laboured for our birth.

December 16

> *"But Mary kept all these things, and pondered them in her heart."*   Luke 2:19

Christmas should cause us to pause and wonder, to revisit what took place over two millennia ago in the little town of Bethlehem. Regarding the Christmas story, the first Christmas story, we read that *"Mary kept all these things, and pondered them in her heart."* Like Mary, we too should meditate over every detail surrounding the birth of Christ. Like a man revelling in his treasure, Christmas should be revelled in and wondered at.

In fact, Christmas should be a time when we dig up and re-examine our "treasures." Just as we take out the ornaments, knickknacks and other decorations in order to prepare for Christmas, so too should we look up and "take out" all the precious truths that surround the Christmas Incarnation for re-examination. The opening chapters of Luke and Matthew should be as familiar and precious to us as the decorations we pull out of the attic.

Unfortunately, because of the busyness of the season and the great crowd of competing events such as deadlines and family visits and school plays and shopping, shopping, shopping, many people leave out the marrow of Christmas, which is Christ. Some only give Him a passing thought. So focussed on the preparations for the turkey, many forget to prepare themselves for the Lamb. For some, the tree eclipses the manger, as they become more concerned with decorating than consecrating. If we are not careful and intentional about it, Christmas can easily become consumed with stress, strife and stuff rather than peace on Earth and goodwill toward men.

Home Alone is a movie I grew up with as a kid. In that movie, Kevin was one of five children. For Christmas the entire family was flying to Paris, France. One problem: in all their preparations, in all their stress, in all their excitement about other stuff, they forgot Kevin at home. Their Christmas ended up being meaningless because they had forgotten to include the most important thing—their child.

Many families—good families—do the same. Overburdened, overtired and overcome by the tyranny of Christmas preparations, some people, instead of pondering Christ and treasuring up the season, rush on from thing to thing, leaving the celebration of the birth of Christ "home alone" while the season passes by.

We need, like Mary, to contemplate the life of our Lord and treasure up all the things He went through in order to redeem us—His humble and humiliating birth, His silent sojourn in Nazareth, His submission to imperfect parents, and above all, His preparation for Calvary. More than a time of giving, more than a time of family, and more than a time of feasting, Christmas above all is a time of worship.

> What grace, what kindnesses, what love
> His mother must have often viewed
> to say to those who had no wine,
> "Whatever He says make sure you do."

December 16

> *"...They said unto him, Rabbi...where dwellest thou? He saith unto them, Come and see. They came and saw where he dwelt..."* John 1:38-39

The High and Lofty One vacated heaven and took up vacancy in time. When Andrew and Simon found Him, He was living somewhere in the vicinity of Nazareth. The plant of renown, the Desire of nations, and the Holy One of Israel chose to live for thirty years in one of the most despised regions of one of the most despised countries of the earth, so great was His love. Nathaniel could hardly believe it. *"Can there any good thing come out of Nazareth?"* he said, astounded they had found the Messiah there (John 1:46).

When God decided to humble Himself, He humbled Himself right down to the very bottom. Not only had He chosen to be a Jew, a despised race of people, weak and hated by the surrounding nations, not only had He chosen to live in despised *"Galilee of the Gentiles"* (Matt. 4:15), a region which many Jews regarded with disdain, but He also chose to dwell in Nazareth, a place we know very little about, but apparently it had quite a bad reputation. In other words, He who deserved the very best resort that earth had to offer ended up staying, figuratively speaking, in a cardboard box on the side of the road.

If this is difficult to imagine, if we have trouble appreciating what our Saviour did for us, let us leave our homes tomorrow to live in the alleys of New York City for a couple of decades. Yet that would not compare with what it must have been like for Him. Let us go even further. Let us go into a foreign culture, where we are despised for the colour of our skin or the language of our voices, and let us live in a ghetto or a shantytown for the rest of our lives. Perhaps then we will begin to see the humiliation and hardship He underwent to save us.

The Lord didn't cut corners either. He experienced all the deprivations and difficulties of life. When He was hungry He did not use His powers to feed Himself bread (Luke 4:3). When He was tired He did not use His supernatural power to refresh Himself, but felt the weariness of His body. He got up early every day and went to work like the rest of us. He grew tired, He grew weary, He felt pain. What irony, what love. The very One who *"fainteth not, neither is weary"* (Isa. 40:28), in the days of His flesh, *"being wearied with his journey, sat thus on the well"* (John 4:6).

Nor did He save Himself from the cross. Our Saviour experienced every hardship in life that He might be a sympathetic and faithful High Priest. When He arose from the dead to enter heaven as the Forerunner for us, He was fully equipped to help us in our greatest time of need.

Across the mountains down He came
To Bethlehem to Nazareth to Galilee
Down to the very lowest place
Gethsemane, Gabbatha, Calvary.

 December 17

> *"And he came to Nazareth, where he had been brought up..."*   Luke 4:16

I grew up watching the old Superman movies, the ones starring Christopher Reeves. I have always been amazed by the back story of Superman, how he came from a distant planet, disguised his identity on planet Earth as Clark Kent, curtailing his power, in order to live a regular life in the farming community of Smallville, Kansas. He submitted to the guidance and wisdom of his earthly parents, Jonathan and Martha Kent, even though his power and abilities were a million times greater than theirs.

Clark Kent reminds me of Jesus of Nazareth. The real man who is super, the Man Christ Jesus, suspended the voluntary use of His powers during His sojourn on planet earth. He did this to identify with me. I live day in and day out without recourse to supernatural abilities. So He did too. Like an empathetic friend who shaves his head bald to show solidarity to someone dying of cancer, my own Saviour shaved off His power in order to empathize with me. Not only does He know everything about me because He is omniscient, but He also knows everything about me because He went through it Himself. How can we not love such a God as He, a God willing to forego so much in order to gain so little?

Let me describe my favourite scene in *Superman 2* to you. At some point in the movie Clark Kent realizes he loves Lois Lane but cannot be with her because of His powers. Then Superman makes the ultimate sacrifice—he gives up His power so that He might pursue a relationship with Lois Lane. After he enters a room on his spaceship that divests him of his supernatural abilities, he and Lois go out for a bite to eat. At the restaurant there is an altercation. A man punches Clark Kent in the face and for the first time, he bleeds. He bleeds for Lois Lane. How beautiful is that?

Our Saviour did the same. He temporarily relinquished the use of His supernatural abilities for a season in order to restore the relationship we lost through sin. He bled. He tasted death. He spent thirty years disguised as a nobody, waiting for the day He would die for me—waiting for the time of separation to be over.

God longs to dwell with His people. He has proven it by going to such great lengths to save them.

> The mountain masked its awesome strength
> to minister to the pebble;
> The king removed his stately robes
> and fraternized with rebels.

December 17

"Let us now go even unto Bethlehem, and see this thing which is come to pass…"   Luke 2:15

Kids sometimes say the funniest things. My son was trying to draw God one time on a page. He paused to ponder and asked, "Dad, what colour is God?" Before I could answer, he beat me to it and said, "Oh, yeah, I forgot. He's lellow."

At Christmas time the kids can say funny things as well. I heard of one boy who thought the shepherds went to "Buffalo Ham" to visit baby Jesus. Another boy, when reciting Isaiah 7:14, said "Behold, a version shall conceive and bear a Son." One enthusiastic boy said his favourite Christmas decoration was the "activity scene" of Mary and Joseph.

But kids can understand profound wonder as well. My heart was filled with worship one morning when I entered my daughter's room after a worried and erratic sleep. To my surprise, all on her own, she had arranged every character and animal of her Nativity Scene to worship at the foot of baby Jesus. All the figurines were amassed together at the front of the manger as if in profound adoration. It looked like a rock concert with Jesus on centre stage. Even Joseph and Mary had taken their place in the crowd. Only Jesus was the focus. Needless to say, my heart swelled up with joy and my eyes misted over as I humbly took my place among the crowd of figurines.

Kids can also understand theology, too. When reading a Christmas book with my daughter the other day she pointed to Mary's belly and said, "God is up in the sky and He is in Mary's tummy, too." I did not bother to inform her that the word for this is "omnipresence." I figured she could learn that later. She also told me that "Jesus was His nickname but God was His real name." I decided not to ruin the moment by labelling it as the "hypostatic union of Christ."

But what she said is important because while the world loves to think about the baby in the manger, it does not like to entertain the idea that God dwelt in the manger. The world wants the cute but rejects the holy. They want "happy holidays" but refuse to acknowledge Jesus in the holidays, or any days for that matter. The world wants a "Merry Christmas" but tries in vain to be merry without Christ.

It is vital we communicate the message of Christmas in our families and Sunday Schools. We must not let the propaganda of Santa Claus win the battle. Be faithful to Him through December. Refuse to lose focus or to allow Christmas to become frivolous. Like the first Christmas night, when the shepherds gathered to worship, it is most holy. Enshrine Christ in the centre of your home; let worship be the spirit of the season. If Christmas doesn't mean anything to us, chances are, it won't mean anything to our children. The children follow our lead.

<blockquote>
Out of the mouth of babes
Praise ascends on high,
Moistening the shrivelled minds
Theology makes dry.
</blockquote>

December 18

"he hath no form nor comeliness…"   Isaiah 53:2

In the dead of winter all the deciduous trees near my house stand naked. All the beautifully shaped leaves are gone. All the brilliant and varied colours of the fall have been stripped bare. Emptied of their glory, the trees stand silent, waiting for the coming of spring. They wait for the time when trees will reign in glory again.

The Lord Jesus Christ was just such a tree. Even though He was the most beautiful tree ever to flourish on the face of the earth, He lived like a tree in winter. Bereft of His outward glory, for the sake of man's redemption and to provide for us an example to follow, the Lord Jesus did not allow His glory to fan out like a peacock's tail but chose rather to empty Himself and live a life of poverty and hardship.

The Apostle Paul summarizes the life of the Lord Jesus in one sentence by saying, *"though he was rich, yet for your sakes he became poor, that ye through his poverty might be rich"* (2 Cor. 8:9). At the end of His life, it seemed all He possessed were the clothes on His back. His quiet life of dormancy lived on the streets and in the shops of Galilee prepared Him to be our example and sacrifice, *"And being made perfect, he became the author of eternal salvation unto all them that obey him"* (Heb. 5:9).

In John Milton's poem on the Nativity, he imagines the Lord born in the season of winter. Milton suggests through his imagery that in order to mimic her Lord, nature laid aside the glory of her beauty, covering it with a thick blanket of snow. Nature blushed to show her beauty while her Lord laid so bare. It was not time for her to dance with her "lusty paramour" called spring. Spring would come with the resurrection of Christ, but until then Nature chose to reflect the mood of her Master.

C. S. Lewis uses the same pathetic fallacy in *The Lion, the Witch and the Wardrobe*. Mr. Tumnus explains that because of the curse it is "always winter, but never Christmas." As a result, all of Narnia lay frozen under the spell of the Witch. But have no fear, the Beavers tell us, "Aslan is on the move." Indeed the Lord Jesus Christ is on the move, and it all began in a manger over 2000 Christmases ago.

Only for a brief moment did the glory of that majestic tree, the Lord Jesus Christ, blossom forth in all its glory. On the Mount of Transfiguration, to only a handful of people, the glory of God shone out from the face of the Lord Jesus Christ. So bright was His light that the noon day sun seemed dim. So white were His garments that normal white seemed soiled and dirty. Then the glory disappeared to wait the time of spring again. Till then we wait, till the Lord Jesus Christ comes again, not to lie in a manger but to sit on a throne of glory.

> Like the moon whose brightness wanes
> so the Lord His glory changed.
> He crammed His bulk into a crib
> and gave Himself that we might live.

December 18

> *"And when they had seen it, they made known abroad the saying which was told them concerning this child."*   Luke 2:17

My wife and I love to see the decorations and displays set up at Christmas time, especially the Christmas lights. Those homes which are choreographed to music or special themes we find most enjoyable. One of the best light displays we ever enjoyed was on a little street named Joysey Boulevard.

Set to the sound of the most popular Christmas carols, channeled through a certain frequency of a local radio station, the whole performance lasted about ten minutes. The entire display was professionally done and the music built up to a resounding crescendo. There was only one problem: the home was located on the end of a cul-de-sac. As a result, the whole street was always packed, and people were always lined up waiting for their turn to see. Needless to say, the neighbours of Joysey Boulevard quickly lost their "joy" after about the first week.

I couldn't help but consider the contrast. On the first Christmas night, when the greatest display of God's revelation and glory was sent into the world, only a few shepherds gathered to see it. Meanwhile hundreds and hundreds of people came every night in my hometown to watch a ten minute light show on a crowded street.

How is it that more did not line up to see the heaven-sent Messiah? It is not as if those shepherds kept the news to themselves. The Scriptures record that they *"made known abroad the saying which was told them concerning this child. And all they that heard it wondered at those things which were told them by the shepherds"* (Luke 2:17-18). It is not clear whether they knocked on doors that very night telling everyone who answered what they had found, or whether they waited until morning to tell everyone they met on the street. Either way, the result was the same. No one listened. No one came to the manger to see the Babe.

I would like to think that the people of Bethlehem got out of their beds and went to the stable that very night, to behold the wonder of which the shepherds spoke. I would like to think that a town hall meeting was called the next day to hear what the shepherds had to say, after which the whole town travelled en masse to see the place where the Child lay. But all this is speculation. No one, as far as we know, went out to see the Wonder of all wonders, the Incarnate God. Just as there was no room for the Saviour in the inn, so too it seems, there was no interest in men's hearts to see the newborn Child.

Such is the world God was born into. Such is the world the Lord came to save. So far the Lord of glory had travelled to seek and to save mankind, but no such effort was made by man to reciprocate. The first Christmas light display was set up in a little town of Bethlehem but only a handful had gathered to see.

> Lord of love, You gave us breath
> Lord of life, You conquered death,
> Lord of light, You heal our eyes,
> Lord of truth, You kill our lies.

# December 19

"And on earth peace..."   Luke 2:14

The angelic host proclaimed peace to the shepherds but what type of peace? Isaiah spoke of a time when men would *"beat their swords into plowshares, and their spears into pruninghooks...neither shall they learn war any more"* (Isa. 2:4). Was this the type of peace the angels announced to the shepherds that night? Was all war to end that night?

There are many types of peace in the Bible. Justification by faith gives us one type of peace. Paul in Romans 5:1 describes this as *"...peace with God through our Lord Jesus Christ..."* Another type of peace is the peace that comes through prayer and trust. In Philippians 4:7 Paul speaks of this type of peace, *"the peace of God, which passeth all understanding,"* which comes to us when we make our prayer requests known to God with thanksgiving (Phil. 4:6-7). Yet there is another type of peace which is the peace of the Millennial reign of Christ. That era will usher in and officially inaugurate socio-economic peace and grant justice to all, and "in His name all oppression shall cease" (*O Holy Night*, Adolphe Adam). When that peace descends there will be no more war.

Zacharias spoke of that peace in the Temple. *"Through the tender mercy of our God"* (Luke 1:78), he said, the Dayspring from on high had come to visit His people. Zacharias prophesied that He, the Christ, would give the *"knowledge of salvation unto his people by the remission of their sins"* (Luke 1:77), and that He would give *"light to them that sit in darkness and in the shadow of death."* Christ would be the One to *"guide our feet into the way of peace"* (Luke 1:79). Through faith, we receive the forgiveness of sins and the gift of eternal life. These are the foundation of all peace.

That first Christmas night, the Seed of our peace was planted in the dry ground of Israel's spiritually bankrupt garden. Tucked away in a manger, outside the inn, the Babe slept, waiting to bring us peace. His peace begins in our life the moment we lay down our disagreement with Him and accept His terms of peace. That's the wonder of it all: the Prince of Peace is willing to make peace with us. All He requires of us is to sign His peace treaty through faith. Are you willing to lay down your sword and shield to make peace with Him?

Isaiah told us that *"Of the increase of his government and peace there shall be no end"* (Isa. 9:7). That peace began Christmas night. That peace begins when you receive Him as Saviour. That peace will expand into the Millennium and all who have trusted Him will rule and reign with Him for a thousand years. Then, and only then, will there be *"on earth peace"* (Luke 2:14). In that day the wolf will lay down with the lamb. In that day everyone will live peacefully under His rule. In that day the world will turn its weapons of war into instruments of agriculture and labour. Oppression shall cease. World hunger shall end. At that time He will reign and *"righteousness shall be the girdle of his loins, and faithfulness the girdle of his reins"* (Isa. 11:5).

> When I sought amnesty,
> Exiled to the cross I fled;
> When I needed asylum,
> Into the empty tomb I crept.

December 19

"...mine ears hast thou opened..."   Psalm 40:6

God the Father gave the Son a body in the virgin's womb so that the Son could sacrifice it on Calvary's altar. Since sacrifices and offerings and the blood of bulls and goats could never take away sin, God provided for *"himself a lamb for a burnt offering"* (Gen. 22:8). In the womb of the virgin, God's divine nature and human DNA combined to present the only begotten Son of God. All the information of divinity lay encrypted in that little Babe, plus all the genetic features of a human being, yet without sin. He was, as the creed states, "very God of very God," a bona fide human being.

The Scriptures are strangely silent about such a significant birth. John describes it as *"the Word was made flesh"* (John 1:14). The Psalmist said, *"mine ears hast thou opened"* (Ps. 40:6). Luke gives us the details, reporting that the Child was found *"wrapped in swaddling clothes, lying in a manger"* (Luke 2:12). Matthew tells us only that Mary *"brought forth her firstborn son"* (Matt. 1:25). Mark doesn't mention it at all. Phillip Brooks captured and expressed the irony of it all in his wonderful carol *O Little Town of Bethlehem*: "How silently, how silently, the wondrous gift [was] given." That body, precious as it was, hardly received any special notice at all.

But He used that body to serve us. The Son of Man came, He said, *"not to be ministered unto, but to minister, and to give his life a ransom for many"* (Mark 10:45). At first, He used that body for work. With Joseph He learned, as every Jewish son learned, to work his father's trade. The Lord knew what it was to work with His hands. The Lord knew hard labour. He had callouses. He knew what it was to get up early and work for a living. Like a farm-raised calf fattened from the stall, the Lord Jesus maintained Himself up to the day He was sacrificed on Calvary's altar.

While the world was perishing, Jesus waited as His body grew. He grew *"in wisdom and stature"* (Luke 2:52). He learned to memorize the Scriptures that spoke of Him. Think of it and marvel: He learned His ABC's, then He learned to speak, then He learned to read. Then He read the Scriptures that spoke of Him. When He was twelve years old, He was found in the Temple *"sitting in the midst of the doctors, both hearing them, and asking them questions"* (Luke 2:46). In Nazareth, as a fully grown man, He attended the local synagogue, *"as his custom was"* (Luke 4:16), and stood up to read.

How long had the Lord of glory been in the midst of their synagogue yet they didn't know it? How many times had the congregation prayed Messiah would come? Yet there He was in their midst, in the second seat, fourth row from the back. When He stood up to read, proclaiming to them the Scripture was fulfilled that day in their hearing, the first phase of his Incarnation was complete (Luke 4:21). His ministry had begun.

<blockquote>
Bethlehem was such a tiny box
To present the Great "I Am."
The infinite immense immortal One
contracted to a span.
</blockquote>

December 20

"Father, glorify thy name. Then came there a voice from heaven, saying, I have both glorified it, and will glorify it again."   John 12:28

The Incarnation glorified the Son. What was meant as humiliation has turned out for glory. He humbled Himself when He took up our likeness, a human nature like ours but without sin. He humbled Himself further, when He took upon Himself the form of a servant and washed our feet. He humbled Himself even further when He was sprawled out on a cross of shame. In all this He was glorified. To be glorified through humiliation is paradoxical indeed, yet that is what the Word of God proclaims.

The Incarnation, first and foremost, brought glory to God, just as the angels proclaimed. Notice also the kind of glory the angels spoke about: glory in the **highest**. Throughout the Old Testament, God had done glorious things—He created the universe in six days, He rescued Israel from the clutches of Pharaoh, He sustained them in the wilderness, He knocked down the walls of Jericho with a shout, etc. In all these "deliverances" God was glorified. But God was glorified **in the highest** when He "delivered" us through His Son. Now He receives glory in the highest degree. In the manger, God truly outdid anything He had ever done.

But the cross glorified Him most of all. It is precisely because He who is so high was born so low that we love Him so much. It is because the Darling of heaven, adored and attended upon by so many, laid aside His glory and lived without comfort thirty plus years in Nazareth that we love Him so. It is because He was willing to be spit upon, arrested like a criminal and stripped naked, even though *"the heavens are not clean in his sight"* (Job 15:15), that our hearts are forever bound to Him.

Though the manger humiliated Him, at the same time it glorified Him. At the bottom of His humiliation, the lowest point, was the cross of Golgotha. There He earned the name that is above every name by taking the lowest name the earth could give Him. His name *"shall be exalted and extolled, and be very high"* (Isa. 52:13), Isaiah prophesied precisely because His name was brought so low, and abased, and extinguished.

The One whose name is goodness was looked upon as an imposter. The Truth they viewed as a liar. They hated the One whose nature is Love. But His shame has been turned inside out. What was intended for suffering has become His glory. A new batch of praise that could never have been uttered had it not been for His abasement has been introduced. His humiliation now forever composes a new song *"To the praise of the glory of his grace"* (Eph. 1:6). Heaven shall stand over and over again with rousing ovations at the sight of His nailed scarred hands.

For all eternity we shall revel in Calvary. The shame that He bore, the thorns that He wore, Calvary glorifies it all. The manger was only the prelude to glory. His cross was the crescendo.

Not many came that night to see
The chubby hands of God,
But when He comes with glory cloud
Then every eye shall see.

December 20

"...and laid him in a manger..."   Luke 2:7

They laid Him in a what? A manger? These words don't shock us all that much anymore. Due to too many Sunday School skits and lullaby songs, they've lost much of their original power. Mary and Joseph would have preferred to lay Him in a bed or in a cradle, but the world had no room for the Son of God.

Perhaps if the manger could have been described as a pig's trough we would better understand the scandal. A feeding bin that horses and donkeys drooled into is what the manger really was.

In May 2013, in the Chinese province of Jinhua, a baby was born under despicable circumstances. A baby known only as "Baby 59" was found stuck in a toilet pipe at the bottom of an apartment building. Apparently, someone didn't want the child or "accidentally" let it slip down the toilet. Thankfully, the landlord heard a baby crying in the downstairs apartment. Rescue workers responded immediately. Because they could not pull the infant from the pipe, they tore the bathroom apart and cut the baby from the pipe. "Baby 59" survived and is doing well to this day.

The birth of "Baby 59" was scandalous, even horrific. So was the birth of Christ, though the Sunday school skits have made us forget. Kings do not deserve to be dumped into mangers. The Lord of lords should not have to be birthed in a cave. The royal Child of heaven should have been wrapped in a robe that filled the Temple, not swaddling rags. Yet our God entered into such a dishonourable birth, willing to be humbled so you and I could be saved.

Though humbly born, Christ was no ordinary child. The baby contained the blood which, when shed, would save the world. So rudely cast out He Himself would stop many from being cast out into outer darkness. No room for Him in the inn, but He has made room for all in heaven. Indeed, there is still room for all in the Inn of heaven—the poor, the maimed, the lame, and the blind—because He Himself had nowhere to lay down His sweet head.

But there will be rooms vacant in heaven, sadly. Rooms that could have been filled. The world had no room for Him then, and many have no room for Him now. The Saviour still stands at the door and knocks, waiting to come in, but He will not enter till you let Him in. He knocks and waits, but there is a day coming when that door will be closed. To those who continue to reject Him He will one day say, *"I know you not whence ye are; depart from me"* (Luke 13:25).

The manger was His extended hand to us; the cross, the furthest reach of His outstretched arm. Manger to cross, He stripped Himself of all His visible glory. Yes, the Darling of heaven became a nameless faceless "Baby 59" in a rescue mission designed to save you. As a helpless babe, receive Him now and be forever saved.

<blockquote>
Beside the rusty implements
Near the fodder and the straw,
There amidst the foul stench
God birthed the Son of God.
</blockquote>

December 21

"Glory to God in the highest..."   Luke 2:14

Three little words: *"...in the highest."* What do they mean? Upon reflection we discover they are not little words at all, but lofty ones and full of meaning. In exchange for His abject lowliness we ought to give Him the highest, fullest, greatest praise we can muster.

There are three ways we can understand the words *"in the highest."* First, it might mean that God received glory in the highest realm, the heavenly realm, as opposed to the earthly, on that night of His coming into the world. Note that *"a multitude of the heavenly host"* (Luke 2:13), not just a few, but a multitude, arrived to give Him glory that first Christmas night. Cherubim, seraphim, angels, archangels, principalities, powers, all were in attendance to witness and announce the incarnation of the Christ. In every neighbourhood, down every street, in every abode, the birth of Christ was heralded in the heavens. With a little imagination we can hear over the intercom throughout the golden street the announcement resounding: "Hallelujah! Christ is born in the city of David tonight! Go quickly! Tell the shepherds, redemption has begun!" Up to that point, the pinnacle of all angelic experience was to witness the birth of Christ. If they sang at creation (Job 38:7), surely they must have danced with joy over the incarnation.

Yet the angelic proclamation could be taken in another sense. The idea could be bound up in the degree of glory the Lord achieved through the Incarnation, which was the highest. Never before in the history of earth, nor in the history of angels, had God so humbled Himself. The furthest He had gone in humbling Himself was *"to behold the things that are in heaven, and in the earth!"* (Ps. 113:6). If it was humbling to the Lord to concern Himself with the events of heaven and earth, how much more humbling must it have been to become one of its citizens?

Imagine what it would be like to be the CEO of a global company. It would be an act of humiliation just to visit and oversee the workers who swept the floors of the factories of your corporation. Now imagine yourself becoming that sweeper! Imagine cleaning the floors and ministering in the lunchroom to the tired, aching workers, and at the same time being treated with contempt. Such is the story of Christmas. Men and angels, let us marvel at the One who crouched so low! "Let loving hearts enthrone Him" (*What Child is This*, William C. Dix).

But perhaps we are to understand the angelic proclamation in yet another sense. Perhaps the idea is "Glory to God to the highest degree." In this sense, the angels are commanding all mankind to give God their "utmost for His highest" (to borrow a phrase from Oswald Chambers). Yet, in the light of the humble circumstances of our Saviour's birth, perhaps we should give our "utmost for His lowest." Loud should be our singing. With all our might we should serve Him. Generous should be our giving. Droplets of praise are a poor exchange for rivers of blessing. Likewise, crumbs of gratitude, dispensed on Sundays only in the form of singing, are an insult to the One who daily spreads a feast for us.

Glory to God in the highest means God should get every ounce of praise due to His name. Fully God gave Himself to us; fully we should give ourselves to Him.

> Let the cherubim and the flies
> Let all the earth and purple skies
> Let all creation's symphony
> Peacock the glory of God.

December 21

*"For unto us a child is born, unto us a son is given...
and his name shall be called Wonderful, Counsellor,
The mighty God, The everlasting Father, The Prince
of Peace."* Isaiah 9:6

It takes more than one name to describe Christ. No one word can describe Him. In total, there are seven names that are used to wrap up the Christmas Child and present Him to us.

First and foremost, He is called **Jesus**, which is Greek for Joshua. The sacred name of Jehovah of the Old Testament had been translated into the sacred name of Jesus of the New Testament. Truly the Word morphed and became flesh. The angel told Mary to call the child Jesus, for *"behold, thou shalt conceive in thy womb, and bring forth a son, and shalt call his name JESUS"* (Luke 1:31). The angel said the same to Joseph saying, *"thou shalt call his name JESUS: for he shall save his people from their sins"* (Matt. 1:21). Mary and Joseph did not search Jewish baby books for cute names for their son. "Jehovah is salvation" was to be His glorious name.

But that's not all. His name was to be **Immanuel** as well, fulfilling the prophecy of Isaiah made several hundreds of years before. Note that it would be the people, not His parents, who would call Him "Immanuel," for it says *"Behold, a virgin shall be with child, and shall bring forth a son, and **they** shall call his name Emmanuel, which being interpreted is, God with us"* (Matt. 1:25, emphasis mine). When people saw Jesus they "saw" God.

His name is **Wonderful**. Not only is His name wonderful as in good and sweet and pure but wonderful in the sense of miraculous, marvellous and mysterious as well. The union of God and Man in one body is truly a Wonder.

His name is **Counselor**. No one is as wise as the kingly Jesus; no one is as gentle as the Good Shepherd. Good counselors are not only rich in wisdom but also in sympathy, empathy and care. Jesus excels them all.

Yet He is mighty. He is the **Mighty God**. The Weakling child is the Mighty God. The Child of peace is the same as the One who *"in righteousness he doth judge and make war"* (Rev. 19:11). Lying in a manger He came to offer peace. Sitting on a white horse He will come to separate the sheep from the goats.

And He is the **Everlasting Father**. He is not God the Father, but He is the Father of eternity. He is the head of all things. We read Him saying in Hebrews *"Here am I and the children whom God has given Me"* (Heb. 2:13, NKJV). He is the One *"Whose goings forth are from of old, From everlasting"* (Mic. 5:2). The Lord Jesus Christ, through His incarnation, has now become our Forerunner, Teacher and Pattern to follow.

Lastly, He is the **Prince of Peace**. To know Him is to know peace. Peace on earth was spoken the night of His birth. Peace in the heart comes to the sinner who repents and believes His gospel. Peace flows into the heart of him who commits everything to Him in prayer, with thanksgiving (Phil. 4:6). Through Him, one day, peace will cover the earth as the waters cover the sea.

> More stunning than scarlet sunset
> Or the soothing sound of shushing shore,
> More welcoming than morning birdsong
> Is the sweet soft sound of Jesus' Name.

 # December 22

"Let us now go to Bethlehem and see this thing..."
Luke 2:15

Shepherd one: "Why us? Why would the Lord appear to us? I don't understand. Why are we the ones to see the birth of the long awaited Messiah? We are despised, defiled, dirty. Who would welcome us into their homes, let us trod upon their floors, and where will we put all our sheep?"

Shepherd two: "I will tell you this. The angel said to us, *'Do not be afraid'* (Luke 2:10). I will tell you this. The angel said, *'There is born to you...a Saviour'* (Luke 2:11). I will tell you another thing. I have been a shepherd my whole life. David, too, was a shepherd, and he was taken from the sheep cote to be ruler and shepherd over all Israel. Maybe the Lord has chosen us to be the first to see what He has done."

Shepherd three: "You both don't know what you are saying. Even if we did go, how could we find a baby in the middle of the night? Intrude into someone's home, sheep in tow, demanding to see the Messiah of Israel? If we were to demand to see anyone's baby in the middle of the night we would be accused of burglary or worse."

Shepherd one: "But this isn't just any baby. Those were angels. You saw the light. You heard their message—*'glory to God in the highest, and on earth peace, good will toward men.'* (Luke 2:14). I think He wants us to see the newborn Messiah. He appeared to Jephthah, didn't he? He was an outcast. He appeared to those four lepers and told them to find the Syrian spoil, to go and tell all Israel. He sent Elisha to the widow of Zaraphath, Joshua to Rahab, David to Mephibosheth. I think we should go. I think the Lord wants us to come."

Shepherd two: "I will tell you this. The Lord has gone down to Abram, appeared to him and told him to go and he went. The Lord appeared to Moses in the bush and told him to go and he went. The Lord now appeared to us with those angels, and though I don't understand it, I want to go and see what it's all about."

Shepherd three: "Very well then. *'Let us now go to Bethlehem and see this thing that has come to pass, which the Lord has made known to us.'"* (Luke 2:15, NKJV).

> The Lord is my shepherd,
> en-mangered in Bethlehem.
> Thy wool and thy gentleness,
> They comfort me.

☾ December 22

> *"For as the heavens are higher than the earth, So are My ways higher than your ways, And My thoughts than your thoughts."*   Isaiah 55:9

Unique are all the ways of the Lord. How unpredictable and unprecedented are all His ways! Out of the littlest town of Bethlehem He brings forth the greatest Ruler the world has even known. Out of the most spoiled of all cities of Galilee for reputation, ill-reputed Nazareth, He raises the most spotless, holy, perfect Man. Out of *"Galilee of the Gentiles"* (Matt. 4:15) He lets shine the purest Israelite of the whole nation—the Lord Jesus Christ.

Truly His ways are higher than our ways. What a marvel, the Engineer of our salvation was able to cultivate our redemption in the most adverse climate. The world flexes its muscles and builds its empires for everyone to see. But the Lord hid Himself in a stable, revealing Himself to less than a dozen people at His birth. Likewise, during His three years of public ministry, He did not march up to Rome, flaunt His powers before the kings of this world, or demand to sit upon their thrones. No, on the contrary, He let Himself be thought of as nothing, as no one. He was *"despised and rejected by men"* (Isa. 53:3).

If an alien were to visit our planet in order to know what the creatures of Earth were like, he would only need to know one thing to capture the nature of all humanity: we crucified our God. That would yield irrefutable evidence of the evil, hostile nature of our planet. No need to show our alien inquirer the quaintness of a family gathered round the tree on Christmas morning. Just show it the "holy" priests and the gawking spectators gathered round the bloodied Man of Calvary.

But what would the alien learn of the nature of our planet's God? No doubt it would expect Him to burn up the place in righteous anger and holy fire. But that is not what the unpredictable God did. Rather than destroying mankind for the murder of His Son, He used his execution to pardon what they had done. In this way, an act of murder was turned into a means of life.

The aliens would be dumbfounded. Their hearts would object. Unable to process the contradiction of such mercy in the face of such sin, they would either flee our planet in incomprehensible shock or fall down in awesome wonder.

At times we become too familiar with the ways of God. We need to become unfamiliar with them again, to view them anew with "alien" eyes. *"To whom then will you liken Me"* says the Lord God. *"Or to whom shall I be equal?"* says the Holy One (Isa. 40:25). *"My thoughts are not your thoughts,"* says the Lord. *"Nor are your ways My ways"* (Isa. 55:8), says the awesome, unpredictable, wonderful, untameable God. Indeed, there is no one like Him.

> Out of the sunny meadows
> Of a rich and spacious heaven
> Into the dark and narrow stall
> He alone did this to save us
> To lift us up He gave up all.

 December 23

"...and laid Him in a manger."   Luke 2:7

"What child is this, laid to rest within my cradled arms? Yesterday this bosom was filled with only hay and feed for donkeys. Today I hold the Son of the Most High God? Oh, my legs are trembling and my arms feel weak. I feel I may not be able to cradle such majestic magnitude as this, such enormous eternity compressed to fit into my manger crib.

Can these little legs bear the weight of His awesome glory? Can it be that these filthy arms are permitted to touch the holy of holies, the One who sits enthroned between the holy cherubim, those guardians of God's glory? How is it that I have been chosen to carry Him, this little manger turned holy ark, to shine forth His glory to all who look upon me? O Lord, to what do I owe this holy honour?

Jesus, did I hear them name Him? The Christ has been born in the city of David this night? Has any wood ever had such an honour as this, to hold this power within an earthen vessel so that *"the light of the knowledge of the glory of God* [may shine] *in the face of Jesus Christ"* (2 Cor. 4:6)? Why would my Lord lay such an awesome privilege on such a lowly vessel as I? Surely there are kings' thrones, temple shrines or holy buildings more worthy? In a great house there are not only vessels of gold and silver, but also of wood and clay, some for honour and some for dishonour. But I am among the least of all Your vessels, Lord, and yet You choose to put Yourself within me. Has ever a creature of Earth enjoyed such privilege?

O just give me, Lord, the opportunity, and I will cleanse myself for Thee. From this day forward I will seek to be a vessel holier for Thee, to cleanse myself from all that defiles, from all that distracts, and all that dilutes my love for Thee, that I might be sanctified and useful for Thee, my Master, prepared and ready for every good work. Let me know, O

Lord, how to possess this vessel in sanctification and honour, not as the rest of the mangers of the world, but set apart and wholly devoted to Thee. For who am I that the Son of the Most High God should dwell in me?

Lord, I resolve to give myself to Thee. The humbling of Yourself has truly humbled me. I love You because You first loved me. I want to serve You because You have enlisted me in the way You want to save the world. *'Here am I; send me'"* (Isa. 6:8).

> The manger blushed to think that she
> Could give her bosom to her Lord,
> To know the One whose head she held
> Was why she had been crafted.

December 23

"Sitting down, they kept watch over Him there."
Matthew 27:36

The manger gave birth to the cross. The swaddling clothes He wore at His birth remind us of the single garment He owned at His death. The manger foreshadowed the cross.

As His life moved forward our Saviour shined brighter and brighter, from the miracle of turning water into wine to the resurrection of Lazarus from the dead. From Bethlehem to Calvary He revealed Himself from glory to greater glory. At the same time, however, His life moved downward in reputation, from the first insinuation that *"He* [was] *out of His mind"* (Mark 3:21, NKJV) to the last accusation, where they said, *"Sir, we remember that that deceiver said, while he was yet alive, After three days I will rise again"* (Matt. 27:63). He went from being ridiculed to rejected, from being cursed to being crucified, the most despicable form of death known to the Roman world. The Lord started out in life as an unknown stranger and ended it a despised outcast. All of this He did out of love for the unworthy.

There are two places He did not belong: one is the manger, the other is the cross. But the contrast could not be greater. In the one place, the hard hearted Jews, in ridicule and detestation, sat down and kept watch of Him **there**; in the other place, the lowly shepherds, in wonder and adoration, sat down and watched over Him **there**. The Lord was humbled first in Bethlehem's manger. He was humbled further still as a despised Nazarene. He was humbled most of all on the cross of Calvary. *"We did esteem him stricken, smitten of God, and afflicted"* (Isa. 53:4). There, the lovely One, the theme of angels' songs, became the *"song of the drunkards"* (Ps. 69:12). All of this He did out of love for the unworthy.

"Again, the kingdom of heaven is like unto a merchant man, seeking goodly pearls: Who, when he had found one pearl of great price,

went and sold all that he had, and bought it" (Matt. 13:45-46). It is not hard to see the heart of our Lord Jesus Christ peeking out from behind the parable. He is the merchant seeking beautiful pearls. Why He finds us beautiful we may never fully comprehend. He is the One who sold all that He had—His comfort, His honour, His praise, His riches, all to show the height and depth and length He would go for us. We are that pearl of great price, not because of any intrinsic value of our own, but because of the value He places upon us and because of the price it cost Him to redeem us.

They sat down and kept watch over Him there, but He, because of the great love wherewith He loved us, hung up there keeping watch over them, that all might believe and none perish.

Into the deepest canyon
our Champion descended
and there cried out.
Now it is finished.

December 24

"But they, supposing him to have been in the company, went a day's journey..." Luke 2:44

There are some days I don't enjoy Christmas, and Christmas Eve morning tends to be one of them. All the stress, all the hubbub, all the last minute running around winds me up so tightly I end up rueing the day I am meant to be celebrating. The crowds crowd my joy. The traffic jams my peace. And sometimes, all the preparations make me forget just what I am preparing for. Needless to say, I am glad when the stores close at 5 or 6 pm and all is calm again, all is bright.

I imagine Joseph and Mary felt the same in their preparations for the Passover feast, an event the size of Christmas, for which they travelled miles and miles every year to celebrate in Jerusalem. On one occasion, we read in Luke chapter two, in all their preparations, in all their planning, they actually left Jesus out of the entire occasion. It wasn't until they spent a full day without Him that they began to think of Him again and realized He was missing.

Don't let what happened to Mary and Joseph that fretful holiday time happen to you. Don't lose sight of Jesus because of the crowds, the clutter and the cramming. Remember this is Jesus' day. Christmas is primarily a time of worship, not "gift-ship." Let us seek to enshrine it as a holy-day and to avoid eroding it into simply a "holiday."

Imagine your wedding day or the wedding day of one of your children. The groom stands on the stage, his smile beaming from ear to ear. He is eagerly awaiting the arrival of his bride. At last she arrives but she is so busy greeting the guests, tending to last minute details, checking her phone and calling the caterer that she doesn't even look at her husband to be! Even at the altar saying her vows she is thinking about the reception and if all the guests will be comfortable. Imagine her again at the wedding supper, flitting around talking with everyone, making sure everyone is well taken care of and having a good time, meanwhile her loving groom sits alone at the front table, neglected. This is what it is like when we leave Christ out of Christmas, when we don't give Him His proper place and attention.

This is His big day. We must not let the tyranny of stuff encroach upon our celebrations. Let nothing take Christmas hostage, demanding payment or ransom to get it back. So many competing ideas and pressures seek to hijack Christmas making it something God never intended it to be. We must be intentional about keeping Christ in the midst.

> The hustle, the noise, the rush
> And the crowds and all the fuss
> Replay that first Christmas Eve
> When they couldn't find room in the Inn.

December 24

"...I live by the faith of the Son of God, who loved me, and gave himself for me."   Galatians 2:20

Oh, the silence of Christmas Eve. There is nothing quite like it. The stillness, the softness, the peace, the rest, all wrapped up in joyous anticipation of the coming day. After the children are all asleep, when the food has been prepared for the following day and the last gift has been wrapped, there is no feeling quite as peaceful as the night before Christmas.

My wife and I have a tradition on Christmas Eve. We always try to watch *It's a Wonderful Life* starring Jimmy Stewart as the beloved George Bailey. If you have never watched this Christmas classic, put it on your list for the coming year. It is the story of a selfless man who loses everything in an effort to help everyone else. On the brink of suicide on account of his ruin, George receives a vision from an angel of what his city would be like had he never lived. Through the vision George realizes how many lives he has touched. In the end, the whole town pays tribute to the man they love so much and who has helped them so many times over the years.

George Bailey is just a small shadow of the Lord Jesus Christ. If we could somehow receive a vision from an angel of what the world would be like had He not come, that vision would horrify us. Without the manger and the cross there would be no salvation for the world. Had not the Lord humbled Himself to become flesh, had He not given that body to be crucified and killed on a cross, the world would be lost to Hell. Christmas Eve is a time to ponder how great a difference knowing Christ has made in our lives.

Under the tree I see so many gifts, but there is a gift I do not see with my eyes. There is a gift under that tree I see by faith. By faith I see *"the Son of God, who loved me, and gave himself for me"* (Gal. 2:20). I see the manger He started in and how He experienced shame and humiliation for me. I see Him living quietly and modestly in disreputable Nazareth as He maintained and nourished His body until it reached maturity. Did He think of me as He worked and sweated all day in His father's shop? Perhaps He did (John 17:20).

Lastly, I see Him bruised and bloodied hanging on a tree for me. I hear Him saying, *"Father, forgive them; for they know not what they do"* (Luke 23:34), and I know He is speaking of me. I read of Him thirsting while He was on the cross and I know He was thirsty for me. With my heart contrite and a broken spirit, I hear Him say, *"My God, my God, why hast thou forsaken me?"* (Matt. 27:46). I know I am the reason.

Holy Jesus, gift of God,
Travelled our unholy sod
To give Himself on that dread cross
to fulfill the promise of Christmas.

December 25

"I have glorified thee on the earth: I have finished the work which thou gavest me to do." John 17:4

From the beginning God had planned to dwell with man. But sin tore that plan apart. Self-will destroyed the home. The Gates of Hell had breached a hole in God's paradise and had turned mankind against the God who made them. Hell's forces had succeeded, it seemed, and turned Utopia, with God dwelling in the midst, into a dystopia filled with curses, sorrow and pain. God regretted He had made man. But God had another plan, as God always does, a plan of restoration and forgiveness, a plan to get back to the original plan—but far better.

God's plan was to smuggle a man into enemy territory. This man would not be an ordinary man. This man would be the Lord from heaven disguised as a mere man. Late at night, while the world slept, God sent down the Second Man, the Lord Jesus Christ, not into a luxurious paradise but into a crowded village that had no room for Him. The first Adam awoke in the midst of the gorgeous garden of the paradise of God, but the last Adam awoke in the noisy cold stable in a manger used for feeding animals. But that did not deter Him. The mission—to restore fellowship between mankind and God—was worth it all. Faintly He cooed and burbled while the gates of Hell howled and shrieked into the night. Finally, the "seed of the woman" had been planted in the soil of time (Gen. 3:15).

Quietly, secretly, God dwelt with the sons of men. Slowly, as a despised Nazarene, He grew up in the streets of Nazareth where no one expected to find Him. In the humble home of Joseph and Mary He quietly learned His "father's" trade. The Architect of the Galaxies genuinely performed the role of a carpenter's son. The Maker of the Universe worked away at making toys and trinkets with the wood and stone He himself had conceived.

It was the perfect cover. No one suspected Him of glory. Indeed, He had suspended His glory so that man could not see Him. That way He was free to be known as a man and to appeal to the hearts and consciences of men. He did not cry out, *"nor raise His voice, nor cause His voice to be heard in the street"* (Isa. 42:2, NKJV), but for thirty years He frequented their synagogues, ate and drank in their homes, attended their weddings, their ceremonies and their festivals in the country of Israel. He grew up before them *"as a tender plant, and as a root out of a dry ground* (Isa. 53:2).

At last, the time came for Him to offer Himself to them again. To them He came to give the Tree of Life. Where the first Adam failed, the Last Adam prevailed. The first Man sinned by taking from the tree, the Last Man never sinned but gave Himself on a tree. At first the Lord had driven man out of the garden, but in these last times God has come back to draw man back into the garden. To as many as receive Him to them He gives eternal life.

The redemption of man is the work the Son of God came to accomplish. In the fullness of time God sent forth His Son into the world. He came. He grew. He waited. At last He gave Himself as the bridge by which we can pass over the fires of judgment, dying so that man may return to the paradise of God, restored and unharmed. Through it all, Christ glorified God on the earth.

> How often He must have watched us all
> With a longing and promise to save,
> Since Eden He'd waited and travelled so far
> To reset the world on its axis.

December 25

> *"And I heard a great voice out of heaven saying, Behold, the tabernacle of God is with men, and he will dwell with them, and they shall be his people, and God himself shall be with them, and be their God."* Revelation 21:3

Christmas is the great precursor to heaven. God had always longed to be with the people He created, *"walking in the garden in the cool of the day"* (Gen. 3:8) with them, just as a father or mother long to be with their own children. But tragedy intervened. Sin snaked its way between us and God. Separated from a holy God, mankind wandered out of the garden into the darkness and has been lost to God ever since.

I love reading stories of adoption reunions. Some people after decades of separation and years of pain finally reunite with their birth mother or parents and live happily ever after. One story I read was of a woman who had been searching for her son for over 40 years. Because of an adulterous affair, the child was given up for adoption. But after repentance and years of searching, mother and child were finally reunited.

God's relationship with us is like that too. Because of sin, our relationship has been broken and disrupted. But God has come through the incarnation of Christ to search for us and bring us to Himself. His Holy Spirit is the adoption agency that helps us to find Him.

To dwell with His people has always been God's intent. The tabernacle in the wilderness, that first temporary abode, was what God first designed in order to be close to His people. Although a thick veil and an elaborate system of sacrifice separated Him from the people, He dwelt in the midst and allowed sinners to approach in a limited and temporary way. Then He built the Temple, a more permanent structure that allowed Jew and Gentile alike to be close to Him. But still access to Him was only partial.

Lastly, He made a living temple of Himself and tabernacled among us in a human body. A temporary dwelling place, the body of Christ gave God access to the people and gave people access to Him. God was free to walk, talk and eat with His creation.

The last veil that separated us was the veil of His flesh. The cross was the final sacrifice needed to remove the veil—permanently. At last, the veil of His flesh was torn. *"It is finished"* (John 19:30) in victory He cried for Himself. Now nothing shall separate us from the love of Christ. On the cross the Lord demolished the last and final veil that separated us from Him. When He died, the veil of the Temple was torn by God Himself, from top to very bottom. It is as if God despised that veil, as if He couldn't wait to get rid of it. Finally in Christ His people were free to freely access Him. Finally God could walk again with His people in the cool of the day.

"It is finished" is what Christ proclaimed from the cross. However, no divine interpretation is given us of what those words mean. Viewed from man's point of view, those three words announced the work of redemption finished. Viewed from God's point of view, on the other hand, those three words meant that the time of separation was finally over. The searching Father is at last reunited with His estranged sons.

God began looking for His sons at the manger. He found them at the cross. The cross is the best adoption reunion story ever told.

> The manger pinned the Serpent's tail
> While the cross smashed in his skull.
> Bethlehem began the finishing blow
> but Calvary conquered the Fall.

December 26

"And Mary said, Behold the handmaid of the Lord; be it unto me according to thy word" Luke 1:38

"Then Joseph being raised from sleep did as the angel of the Lord had bidden him, and took unto him his wife..." Matthew 1:24

Mary and Joseph stand out as excellent examples of obedience in the New Testament. They both resolved to obey their Lord but their obedience manifested itself in different ways.

In Mary's case, she resolved obedience from its inception. Like Abraham of old, Mary received a direct communication from the Lord God Almighty telling her specifically what to do, although in Mary's case an angel communicated that message. She was to be a vessel of gestation for her Lord and although she did not understand, like Abraham, she obeyed. Mary had prepared her heart to obey whatever the cost. Mary literally embodied the appeal made to every believer in Romans 12:1, *"that* [we] *present* [our] *bodies a living sacrifice, holy, acceptable unto God, which is* [our] *reasonable service."*

Joseph, on the other hand, shows us the other side of obedience. Determined to "divorce" Mary due to what he considered adultery and fornication, Joseph was interrupted in his plans and told to do the opposite. He was to take Mary as his wife. The Child conceived by the Holy Spirit was not conceived by sinful means. Joseph heard the correction of his Lord and obeyed. Whether one decides to obey from the beginning with prompt obedience, like Mary, or respond to correction, like Joseph, the result is the same.

The truth is, obedience involves a little bit of both. I am sure Joseph at some point had resolved in his heart to obey the Lord with all his mind, soul and strength. Seeking to be obedient to the Law, which said to put away the adulterous woman, Joseph desired to walk in accordance with what he understood from the revealed Word. But God intervened. Taking Mary as his wife was not disobedience to the Law, the angel said. This Child was of the Holy Spirit. Joseph immediately corrected his course and obeyed.

Each one of us ought to dedicate our bodies, like Mary did, to be living sacrifices on the altar of service and give them to the Lord. "Behold, the servant of the Lord" should be the first words we speak every morning. Perhaps the Lord wants to use our bodies to serve within the local church. Perhaps He wants to send our bodies to foreign lands to spread the gospel to those who sit in darkness. Perhaps He wants to use our hands to wash the feet of others in our own community.

Yet each one of us needs to be sensitive, like Joseph, to the gentle correction of our Lord as well. Being finite, being flawed, we often "think" we know the will of God, but God is greater than our piddly minds. He clarifies our understanding. He rewrites our plans. He redirects our steps. We need to change our course if the good Captain of the ship desires to steer us in a new direction.

> Man prepares his plans
> But God directs his steps,
> Man prepares the heart
> But God unfolds the tongue.

December 26

> *"And they were both righteous before God, walking in all the commandments and ordinances of the Lord blameless."*   Luke 1:6

The Lord spoke this statement over the life of Zacharias and Elizabeth. They were righteous before God and blameless in the eyes of men. O how rewarding it would be to have this statement spoken over our lives! Truly great were the men and women who walked blamelessly in all the commandments and ordinances of the Lord. Alexander, Augustus Caesar, Napoleon, all the "greats" of the world, are nothing compared to the greatness of those who obey God's commandments.

Ask a child under the age of 4 whether he would rather have a chocolate bar or a one hundred dollar bill. In my experience the child takes the chocolate bar every time. According to his facile value system a chocolate bar is worth way more than a piece of paper. After all, you can't eat paper. So it is with the value systems of this flawed world. According to their facile system, the man or woman who builds the greatest empire or kills the most enemies is recorded in history as one of the "greats." The world pins medals on the puny while placing dunce caps on the truly great.

Without the gospels the world would be completely ignorant of Zacharias and Elizabeth, yet they were among the worthiest of the earth. Not many tombstones can truly advertise: "Here lies a man who walked in all the commandments of the Lord, and was blameless." From the Old Testament, Samuel was able to say it, declaring, *"Behold, here I am: witness against me before the LORD, and before his anointed: whose ox have I taken? or whose ass have I taken? or whom have I defrauded? whom have I oppressed? or of whose hand have I received any bribe to blind mine eyes therewith? and I will restore it you. And they said, Thou hast not defrauded us, nor oppressed us, neither hast thou taken ought of any man's hand"* (1 Sam. 12:3-4). From the New Testament, the Apostle Paul could say it. At the end of his life he was recorded as saying, *"I have fought a good fight, I have finished my course, I have kept the faith"* (2 Tim. 4:7). Although these men were relatively unknown in the world, they were very well known to God and made it into the greatest history book of the world.

This is the extended family into which the holy Lord Jesus was born. His mother Mary had a strong connection with godly Elizabeth and went to her for advice during the first trimester of her pregnancy. Mary, the handmaiden of the Lord, Joseph the righteous, and blameless Aunt Liz and Uncle Zach were the instructors, guardians and teachers of the holy child Jesus. They were blameless teachers; He was the perfect student. For thirty or more years they ate their meals and served God together in humble Nazareth, unseen by the historian's eye but pleasing to Him who sees all things perfectly.

> Greater is he that is known to God
> Than he that is loved by the masses;
> I rather be the theme of angel's song
> Than known as the smartest, strongest or fastest.

December 27

"And he said unto him, If thy presence go not with me, carry us not up hence."   Exodus 33:15

Catch the vision of the one-eyed preacher from Wales, Christmas Evans. At the age of nine, Christmas Evans lost his father. When the family broke up, Christmas Evans went to live with his alcoholic uncle. As a result, Evans ended up living a life of debauchery, associating himself with gangs, booze and violence. Destitute, delinquent and unable to read, his life appeared to be going downhill fast.

But then the evangelist David Davies came to town. Christmas Evans was converted by the message Davies proclaimed. He then became a mentor to Evans and taught him how to read. In time, he taught him how to preach. Soon Christmas Evans was reaching out to the very gangs with which he used to run. As a reward for his labours, they beat him and gouged out his right eye. But it didn't matter. Evans had already determined in his heart to be single-eyed for Christ, and Christ alone.

Evans preached wherever he went. Without money and without a horse, he criss-crossed the Welsh countryside preaching in churches and open fields to coal miners and churchgoers alike. Revival swept through the land whenever and wherever he preached. So powerful and widespread was his preaching that historians give Evans the name "Bunyan of Wales."

But then, something went wrong. Evans wrestled with health issues, battled false teaching and waves of discouragement. As a result, he determined to scale the Welsh mountains, get alone with God, and not come back down until his spiritual zeal returned.

After a few hours of intense prayer, Evans felt his prayer was answered. He descended from the mountain revived by the Spirit of God. As a result he penned 13 resolutions to follow Christ. The following is his eighth resolution: "I come unto thee, beseeching thee to be in covenant with me in my ministry. As thou didst prosper Bunyan, Vavasor Powell, Howell Harris, Rowlands, and Whitefield, O do thou prosper me. Whatsoever things are opposed to my prosperity, remove them out of the way. Work in me every thing approved of God, for the attainment of this. Give me a heart 'sick of love' to thyself, and to the souls of men. Grant that I may experience the power of thy word before I deliver it, as Moses felt the power of his own rod, before he saw it on the land and waters of Egypt. Grant this, for the sake of thine infinitely precious blood, O Jesus, my hope, and my all in all! Amen."

As this Old Year winds down and the fresh coming New Year starts up, let us examine ourselves to see if we haven't lost our zeal for God and souls. Let us get alone with Him in a quiet place and pray to Him to stoke our hearts until they are burning hot with determination to live for Him. Let us pray, along with the one-eyed preacher, that we may be given a heart "sick of love" for our Lord Jesus Christ. Like Moses of old let us go into the New Year praying, *"If thy presence go not with me, carry us not up hence"* (Ex. 33:15).

> Wood on wood on wood
> I'm building a rescue fire,
> And God sees my prayers.

December 27

> *"But God hath chosen the foolish things of the world..."* 1 Corinthians 1:27

For the Christian, fiction often illustrates reality. I grew up watching the 1964 Christmas classic *Rudolph the Red-Nosed Reindeer*, when one foggy Christmas Eve Rudolph with his nose so bright saved Christmas. Since then, I have watched it many times with my own children. As a child the movie fascinated me for fantastical reasons but now, as an adult, the movie intrigues me as a spiritual illustration of a divine truth.

The divine truth I am speaking of is God's love and interest in misfit things. Rudolph doesn't fit in with the other reindeer because of his misfit nose. In the subplot, Hermey the elf doesn't fit in with his peers either because he wants to be a dentist. The two of them run away together finding solace and belonging on the Island of Misfit Toys.

The Island of Misfit Toys is a place where misfit toys go who don't exactly "fit in" and therefore cannot be given away as gifts at Christmas. On the island Rudolph encounters a water gun that squirts jelly, a polka dot elephant, a doll who feels she is unlovable, and a train with square wheels. Ironically, it is on the island that Hermey and Rudolph find their sense of belonging and usefulness.

Because of the fog Christmas was almost cancelled, but because of Rudolph's unique gift—his bright red nose—Christmas was surely saved. Just as Santa realized the value of Rudolph's unique gift for a specific time and purpose, so too, God has custom designed each one of us and uses our unique individuality for the work of building His kingdom. The truth is, there are no "misfits" in God's Kingdom. Misfits fit perfectly well into the plan of the wise Master who uniquely created them in the first place.

God has placed each believer in the body of Christ as He saw fit (1 Cor. 12:11, 18). The body of Christ is composed of many parts, but we are one body in purpose (Rom. 12:4-5). One is an eye, one is an arm; one has the gift of smelling, another the gift of hearing (1 Cor. 12:15-17). We all have a special gift and a specific role to play. Diversity is not our weakness; it is our strength. Diversity, not bland conformity, has always been God's way.

In the end, Santa comes to the Island of Misfit Toys in order to deliver each toy to a specific boy or girl as a blessing for Christmas. This delightful fiction reflects a divine reality: in His time, God will take up our unique gift and personality and use it as a blessing in someone else's life. To God be the glory.

> I may be the foot
> But don't look down on me;
> I am one of His glorious feet,
> and how beautiful they are.

December 28

"And she said unto her husband, Behold now, I perceive that this is an holy man of God, which passeth by us continually. Let us make a little chamber, I pray thee, on the wall; and let us set for him there a bed, and a table, and a stool, and a candlestick: and it shall be, when he cometh to us, that he shall turn in thither. And it fell on a day, that he came thither, and he turned into the chamber, and lay there."
2 Kings 4:9-11

Behold, the famous unknown woman of Shunem who Elijah went to visit! Her choices and actions were noticed by God but unnoticed by men—so notable that the Lord has decided to parade her actions throughout history wherever the Bible is read. Like Mary, who poured out her alabaster jar of ointment as an act of adoration and worship, whose actions were recorded for all time in the Scriptures, so too, the notable Shunemite woman's love was recorded for all to see, though she herself had no idea she was setting an example for the world to follow.

The Greeks made statues to commemorate their notable citizens, erecting statues and busts in public places or sacred shrines. In Rome they gave men of renown a triumph as all the city lined the streets to mark their return. In our part of the world, the West, and in our day and age we recognize excellence by awarding the notable people of Earth with Nobel prizes in the categories of science, art or world peace. But what does the God of heaven think? He celebrates greatness by immortalizing acts of faith and sacrifice in the pages of His eternal Word, in order that all who read may be their imitators.

So it is with our actions. As we serve the Lord Jesus in our local churches, in our hometowns, in our respective jobs, we have no idea how far our influence may extend. Our demeanour in the home may set the tenor for generations to come, influencing our children to the third and fourth generations. Our commitment to the local church may result in the healing and health of several families beyond our own. Our testimony at work, observed in secret by some, in public by others, may end up being the catalyst that brings about someone's repentance and thirst for God. How far the ripples extend we may never know. We sow in hope.

The New Year holds many opportunities. Some will appear as the days unfold. Others we must prepare for by determining how to use our time and resources for the building up of His Church and the extension of His Kingdom. Gladys Aylward saved up the little money she earned every day until she had enough money to buy a one-way ticket to China, where she served as a missionary to the end of her life. Hudson Taylor began preparing his mind and body for the mission field by living on rice alone and studying the Chinese language every day. What are you preparing for in the coming year?

Let us have a mind like the woman of Shunem and prepare something now — the house we live in or the money we save, in order to give it to some noble cause — a noble cause that may hold influence for all eternity.

> Here's my heart, Lord, take and plant it
> And water it with all my tears;
> Like Moses plough me in the desert
> That I may serve you all my years.

December 28

"Then David the king stood up upon his feet, and said, Hear me, my brethren, and my people: As for me, I had in mine heart to build an house of rest for the ark of the covenant of the LORD, and for the footstool of our God, and had made ready for the building."

1 Chronicles 28:2

What should be the attitude of our heart heading into the New Year? May I suggest we adopt the same attitude as our spiritual father David, who had it in his heart to do something for the God he so loved? Many may have plans for their finances, their homes or vocations in the coming year, but who among us has planned it in his heart to do something big for God?

David had big plans for God. After having spent twenty or more years running around the Judean countryside trying to escape the fierce jealousy of Saul, after spending another half a dozen years consolidating the kingdom after Saul's demise and defending it from imposters to the throne, David did not take up the easy life. He certainly could have. But instead he took up a new project for God and began making preparations for the Temple.

When David's persecutions were over, when all the running and fighting was done and God had given him rest from all his enemies, what did David do? Did he relax and enjoy the newly established peace of his kingdom? Did he take a long sunny vacation or pursue some hobby like hunting or fishing? No, as soon as David's trials were over, he immediately began the work of building the Temple of God. In one sense, David had already done enough. God had called him to be a king, and that promise, twenty years later, had come to pass. To sit on the throne of Israel was a major accomplishment of faith in and of itself. If anyone had a "right" to sit around and take it easy, it was David.

Even though David was not allowed to build the Temple (for that honour was to be given to his son, Solomon), he still did not stop making preparations for the building of the Temple. Some of us may be called to be missionaries in foreign lands. Some of us may be called to be shepherds of churches. Some may be called to be teachers. But that should not stop each and every one of us from making preparations to do the same. Study the Word of God as **if** you were going to be a teacher or preacher. Sanctify yourself, above reproach, as **if** you were called to be a shepherd of the flock. And dedicate yourself with all your heart, soul and mind, as **if** you were going to leave your homeland to be a missionary in a foreign field in the coming year.

Be ready and prepared for what God may call you to do. Seek to live on a higher plane with God. Live simply, and be ready to relinquish all you own in order to live as a missionary in a foreign land. Be eager, like David, to do something great for God, not to make a name for ourselves, but to see His name exalted and honoured among the nations.

> Build a temple, for God, build a tower,
> Each day yield, a brick, a mortared hour
> That all who see, the Temple, see
> We serve with all our mind, love, power.

December 29

"...it shall bruise thy head, and thou shalt bruise his heel."   Genesis 3:15

As we approach the end, let us go back to the beginning. In the beginning God created the heavens and the earth. Why? What was the purpose of it all? In the end, how is this thing called "history" going to culminate?

The crown, climax and culmination of creation was the making of man in God's own image in order that He might have a relationship with mankind. Adam, the head of the human race, and Eve, his beloved helper, were brought into the world to share in the glory and knowledge of God. God is so gracious to share Himself with us. What a glorious privilege He has birthed us into! If those who are born in the West consider themselves to have been born into privilege, how much more those who have been born again into the riches of His inheritance? Oh, that our eyes could see it! (Eph. 1:18).

But sin quickly made a mess. Adam took of the tree, smashing glass and spreading acid everywhere. He pressed the button and the atomic bomb of sin went off in our world. We know we live in a post-apocalyptic world. But no worries, God knew it was going to happen and planned for it. His ultimate plan marches on despite our sin. Even though we messed up, God had a secondary fail-safe plan by which to bring redeemed sinners into a permanent relationship with Himself. God will get what He wants one way or another. He is unstoppable!

The fail-safe plan was Christ, the Creator Himself, sent down to enter the human race as a son of Adam for the sons of Adam in order to bring the sons of Adam to God. He is still in the process of carrying out that plan. Christ is the original and only rescue plan. This space station, planet Earth, has been irreparably damaged and only those who board the rescue shuttle, the Lord Jesus Christ, will escape the destruction.

It all began in the Garden of Eden with that first special promise concerning the Seed of the woman which would bruise the Serpent's head (Gen. 3:15). That promise continued through the families of Abraham, Isaac and Jacob, through whom *"all families of the earth be blessed"* (Gen. 12:3). That promise continued until one of the descendants of Jacob gave birth to the promise and laid Him in a manger. That promise continued when they crucified Him and laid Him in a tomb. That promise continued when God raised Him from the dead and seated Him at His own right hand until His enemies become His footstool (Heb. 10:13). That promise continues to this day!

At Christmas time we remember the Last Adam that came into the world, born not in a paradise but into a barren sinful land, welcomed not by an admiring nation but rejected by His own people. Looking back, it has been over 2000 Christmases and we still await the return of the Lord from heaven (1 Thess. 1:10). When He comes, in that Day, He will be gloried in and admired among all those who believe (2 Thess. 1:10).

The fulfillment of all things is at hand. Messiah's heel is raised and soon Satan's head will be crushed. The final blow approaches. The table is set and the marriage supper is nearer than when we first believed. *"But the end of all things is at hand: be ye therefore sober, and watch unto prayer"* (1 Pet. 4:7).

Christ the kernel, Christ the seed
Christ the flower, Christ the tree;
Christ the fallen, Christ the risen
Christ the coming Lord from heaven!

December 29

"...the words that I speak unto you, they are spirit, and they are life."   John 6:63

Reading the Bible is not just an academic exercise. It is a life giving experience. It is like sunlight to a flower. It causes you to develop, produce fruit and grow. The Word of God is food and reading it is like eating food. It sustains our spiritual lives and gives us strength to do the will of God. To neglect the Word of God is to choose to wither, weaken and wane.

It is wise to read the Word of God. January is a great time to get motivated to read the Word of God again. To read the Bible systematically all the way through from cover to cover is something every new Christian must do. If you have not already done that, I would suggest putting down this book and reading the Bible straight through for the next 40 days until you are finished. If that task seems too daunting, take as many days as you need. There are many daily reading plans that can help us consume the full meal of His Word.

I find there are three things necessary to read the Word of God. First, we need to have a plan. Plan the work and work the plan is a good motto to live by. Determine to read a certain number of chapters of the Bible per day. There are other goals we set in life, such as saving money or setting aside time to spend with our kids, and we do this because we know these things will not happen unless we schedule them in. The Word of God is much too important to be read at random. Put God's Word in your calendar each day.

The second thing necessary for reading God's Word is setting aside a designated time and place to read. This can be an actual physical place, like an office or a rocking chair by a window. Or it can be a designated time like the morning or the evening. Whatever the setting, whenever the time, let it be a time and a place that is quiet and without disturbance. Hang a "do not disturb" sign on the door of your heart and enter alone into a space with God. Get away from the demands and rush of the day to listen solely to the Commander of the Day.

Lastly, we need a purpose. Why are we reading the Word of God? Are we reading it because "we are supposed to?" Are we reading it to brag to others that we have read it all the way through? Or are we reading it to enjoy and to follow the living God, our heavenly Father who loves us and wants to bless us? In other words, are we reading to worship? Read to get to know Him. Enjoy sitting on your heavenly Father's lap while He speaks to you. Lay your head on His bosom and hear His voice. Determine to imitate whatever it is He whispers in your ear.

After reading His Word—after getting down from His lap, so to speak—live out the day like children who play while their parents watch over them from nearby. Know that your heavenly Father is watching over you, guiding you, and protecting you, as you complete the tasks He has given to you. Make the adjustments to your character which He has revealed to you. Go in the strength of your Father's love.

> With His finger in the dust
> our Lord wrote on the ground,
> for only those who draw in close
> can know what He wrote down.

December 30

"And Jesus said unto him, Why callest thou me good? there is none good but one, that is, God."
Mark 10:18

A Good Man is Hard to Find is the title of a short story written in 1953 by Flannery O'Connor. The story challenges us to think long and hard about what it means to be a good man. Every character in the story is flawed, and thus it is hard to find a good man in the story. The father is sour; he is curt and stern with the closest members of his family. The mother, sitting in a stupor, apathetic to what's going on in her home, becomes complicit in the father's sins. The children are no saints either — in fact, they appear to be nothing more than spoiled brats. Even the grandmother, the protagonist of the story, despite all her moralizing and reminiscing about the good ole days when people acted more decently, reveals her own selfishness and manipulative ways by the end of the story. In fact, the antagonist of the story, an ex-con dubbed by the media as "The Misfit," is obviously flawed, but at times appears more righteous than even the victims he is tyrannizing. After reading the story one feels that truly a good man is hard to find.

God must feel the same when He looks at planet Earth. David, a man acquainted with righteousness, said it well when he penned the verse, *"And enter not into judgment with thy servant: for in thy sight shall no man living be justified"* (Ps. 143:2). The undeniable truth is, we are all flawed. One is flawed with murder, another with hate. One is flawed with adultery, another with lust. One is flawed with thievery, another with covetousness. This one is an angry man; that one is proud. This one is vain; that one is gluttonous. Only if God ranks these sins as first, second and third degree can we assess ourselves as better than others. But God does not rank sin. It is all rank to Him.

So what are we going to do in the coming year? Since it is impossible to be righteous and good in His sight should we just give in to our sinful urges and live like the animals? The Apostle John seemed like a good man. James, the brother of Jesus, went down in history as an example of a "holy" man. Countless missionaries have given their lives in service and ultimately in death for the sake of others. Is it possible for bad sinners to be good men and women for God?

Through the Holy Spirit, says the Word of God, it is possible—triumphantly possible. In fact, Jesus came in order to make bad sinners good. He has called us the light of the world, and through our actions people will glorify our Father in heaven because of us (Matt. 5:16). The world will know we are His disciples if we have love for one another (John 13:35). If it were not possible for us to be good, then these statements of our Lord would make no sense.

The truth is, a good man is difficult but not impossible to find. Yes, we are sinners and yes, we still have a sinful nature. But the greater truth is that in Christ we are a new creation. In Christ, a new man—a good man—can be found. The Holy Spirit dwells within us to empower us to live good and righteous lives for God's glory.

> Why do you call me good?
> Only one is good and that is God.
> But in us dwells One who is good
> And from us makes His goodness shine.

December 30

"...freely ye have received, freely give."
Matthew 10:8

We are all like the children from Roald Dahl's classic story, *Charlie and the Chocolate Factory*. Willy Wonka, owner of an international chocolate factory, granted five golden tickets to five undeserving children, inviting them to visit and see the inner workings of his factory, and to learn the secrets of his great candy industry. His motive, unknown to the children, was to find someone worthy to take over and inherit the operations of his great empire. In the end, all the children proved disqualified except one. Of all the children, only Charlie Bucket passed the test.

The disciple's goal is to be like Charlie Bucket. As we serve the Lord on the earth, may we all be found to be faithful. The Lord Jesus Christ has given us an invitation to join Him in His great work to save *"whoever believes"* (John 3:16, NKJV). Ours is the privilege to pattern our lives after His example and to herald His Word with the preaching of our lips and lives. Let us not be like the children in Dahl's story who squandered away their opportunity by living for themselves, trying to get all they could out of the "sweets" of this life. One by one the children lost the opportunity to receive the inheritance of the Chocolate Factory.

When the Lord returns, perhaps this coming year, He will settle accounts with His servants. He will be looking for that faithful and wise steward who looked after His Master's things (Luke 12:43). He will evaluate the way we used the deposit He left with us, the deposit which was committed to our trust (1 Tim. 6:20). A good return for His investment our Master seeks. Freely we have received, and the Lord will want to know if freely we have given. When the Chief Shepherd returns, He will inspect the way the sheep have been treated and will judge between them, and His judgment will be true, for *"Righteousness shall be the belt of His loins, And faithfulness the belt of His waist"* (Isa. 11:5, NKJV).

We have been given a once in a lifetime opportunity—a golden ticket, if you will. An opportunity has been entrusted to us, and through Him we are to invest in planet Earth. We are to redeem the time, turning time into service for our Master. The Master of the Factory, the Lord of the Harvest, the Captain of the Search and Rescue Vessel is looking for one thing: our faithfulness.

Ponder the question of Solomon's ancient proverb: *"Most men will proclaim every one his own goodness: but a faithful man who can find?"* (Prov. 20:6). Let us examine ourselves much in preparation for our last examination. Let us inspect every corner of our lives in anticipation of the great and final inspection.

The time is short; redeem it now.
There is no free time.
Quickly, Time is
running
out.

December 31

"Therefore, if anyone is in Christ, he is a new creation; old things have passed away; behold, all things have become new." 2 Corinthians 5:17

The month of January is named after the Roman god "Janus." The idol that represents him portrays two faces, one pointing forward to the future, and the other looking back toward the past. January is like a two-edged sword: it causes us to look back over the months that have come and gone while driving us forward to think about the year ahead.

Deep in the dead of winter, January comes to us as a type of spring—a time when all things become new again. To the Christian every month can be like January, a time when we can start again, so to speak, because we serve a God who forgives the past and prepares us for the future. Like flowers after the winter, new shoots spring up in our lives when we start over with God. If anyone is in Christ, he is a new creation—regardless of the month. January serves to remind us of this great truth—if we have forgotten it—as does spring, Monday mornings, birthdays, and back to school Septembers.

The Lord uses these times of reflection to spur us on to love and good works. *"Consider your ways"* (Hag. 1:5). He spoke through the prophet Haggai to the apathetic survivors of the captivity in order to awaken them from their slumber. *"Let us search out and examine our ways, And turn back to the LORD"* said the writer of Lamentations after the destruction of Judah by the Babylonians to lift them from their dejection (Lam. 3:40, NKJV). Reflection should lead to re-examination, which should lead to repentance, which produces reformation, which produces character, which is the goal of everything.

The New Testament also calls for self-examination and directs us toward self-judgment, promising us that *"if we would judge ourselves, we should not be judged"* (1 Cor. 11:31).

The Lord is not a Vice-Principal who delights in giving his students detentions, suspensions and expulsions; rather, He is like a patient father who continues to pursue us until we learn how to do things right. May the Lord give us a trusting heart like the Psalmist's who said, *"Search me, O God, and know my heart...see if there be any wicked way in me, and lead me in the way everlasting"* (Ps. 139:23-24).

No one embodies the spirit of self-examination better than the anonymous writer of Psalm 119. *"I thought about my ways,"* said the resolute Psalmist, *"And turned my feet to Your testimonies"* (Ps. 119:59, NKJV). Clearly, a little reflection goes a long way. January is the right time for reflection because every month is the right time for reflection.

Though some dislike the idea of "New Year's Resolutions," there is a place in the Scriptures calling us to reflection, repentance and resolution. For some, January provides the needed catalyst for the process. To me, whatever the reason and whenever the season, it is always good to resolve to follow the Lord more vigorously.

> I've traced out my steps and thought on my ways,
> I've counted my years and reckoned the days;
> I've thought of my life and planned till the grave,
> from now I will be Thy servant and slave.

December 31

"...lo, I am with you always, even to the end of the age."   Matthew 28:20, NKJV

New Year's celebrations should characterize the entire life of the Christian—not just one day. I use New Year's Eve to remind myself again of the great *"newness of life"* (Rom. 6:4) that I have been born (again) into. I use the time to reflect upon and re-evaluate the golden opportunity that has been granted to me to live for Him, once in a lifetime, for a full life time.

With December, November, October, September, etc. receding in the rearview mirror and January fresh on the horizon, I muse upon all that the Lord has done the previous year. This is a good heart exercise and a biblical one (Ps. 92:2), as it causes the heart to overflow with a good theme. There is something truly good about every reflection—something redemptive to the heart and instructive to the mind—and those who engage in it are wiser for it. Those who live month to month and year to year without reflection are like a man with a head trauma who can't remember. Unreflective Christians run the risk of losing the wisdom they could have gained by a little recollection and review.

Through the difficulties, the Lord has been with us and will be with us. "Through it all, through it all, I've learned to trust in Jesus," the hymn writer said, "I've learned to trust in God" (*Through it All*, Andrae Crouch). Like a good coach in the corner of the ring, the Lord encourages us in times of stress and strife, when our hearts are wrung with grief, to come to Him for a little counsel and refreshment, to have our wounds bandaged and stitched up so we can last another round in the ring. Think how many times the Lord has inspired or assisted you to not give up, but to keep on fighting, to get back in the ring, to hang on, to try again or to keep going.

Through the seasons of sorrows and periods of pain, praise God they are only seasons. Praise God they are only periodic. Yes, *"weeping may endure for a night, But joy comes in the morning"* we are promised (Ps. 30:5, NKJV). And God does not renege on His promises! By faith joy will come in the morning. Your mourning will turn into dancing. Hold on to that and let the Lord hold onto you. The Lord has seen us through the years and He will see us through the next, using the arms of His saints to comfort us with hugs, or speaking quietly to us through the tender times of prayer, somehow letting us know He is there. Many times a timely insight from His Word is all that was needed to buoy us up, far above our sharp and bullying circumstances.

Take heart, child of the Most High, every groan you make is known and duly noted. Every loss will be compensated. Every tear stored up in a bottle (Ps. 56:8). Reflect upon these things and the Lord will give you wisdom. May the Lord truly give you a "New" Year.

> Put your hand in My hand,
> cause I've seen what tomorrow brings.
> Put your heart in My heart,
> for I know that sorrow can sting.
> But put your finger in my Hand
> and your hand in My Side,
> and until the long cold night ends
> beside Me, within Me, upon Me, abide.

OTHER BOOKS BY SHANE JOHNSON

31 Days at Bethlehem's Manger
A Christmas Devotional
Volume 1

The manger contained the cross just as the acorn contains the oak. It was just a matter of time. When the Lord gave His Son by birth, it was in order to give His Son in death. The crucifixion was the incarnation brought to maturity. Conversely, the incarnation was the preparation for the crucifixion. It took 33 years to grow that mighty tree and only six hours to fell it. Three days later the "tree" had sprouted again and spread out all its branches to fill and bless the earth.

See the One whom the heavens cannot contain, pocketed in a manger stall! See the One, the train of whose robe fills the temple, wrapped in swaddling rags! See the One who dwells between the cherubim of glory, dying between two despicable thieves! Let us bow down and marvel, for this is our God.

9781926765686 • 138 pages

Wisdom for Fools
101 Proverbs to Live By

The theme, the thesis and the warning of the book is found right at the beginning, in Proverbs 1:7: *"The fear of the Lord is the beginning of knowledge, but fools despise wisdom and instruction."*

The rest of the book is an expansion of this theme. Those who fear the Lord will humbly read this book. Those who don't fear the Lord live their lives without it. It is humility that keeps a man or a woman reading and rereading this book. Those who realize they are fools in need of wisdom will run to feed from its pages. Those who realize they are paupers will revel in the gold found within the pages of the proverbs.

Whoever memorizes and lives by the proverbs will gain a deep understanding of life and people and will avoid the many hardships and heartaches that foolishness brings. This little book that I have written, which contains 101 proverbs in total, is only a small sample from the rich reservoir of wisdom that is ours to draw from.

9781927521502 • 220 pages

Strength for the Journey
52 Devotions from John Bunyan's *Pilgrim's Progress*

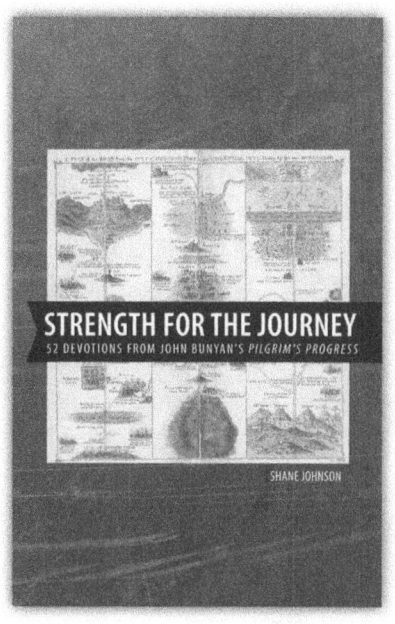

The *Pilgrim's Progress* by John Bunyan has been a source of encouragement for Christians for almost four centuries now. Lately, however, it has fallen out of style. Most Christians under the age of thirty have not taken the time to read this great classic, and sadly, some have never even heard of it. Yet a hundred years ago there was not a Christian in the Western World who was not intimately familiar with Christian and his journey to the Celestial City. Brothers and sisters, this ought not to be so. This little devotional attempts to revive a new interest in The Pilgrim's Progress by explaining some of its most treasured metaphors and analogies. If successful, this devotional will inspire you to read or re-read Bunyan's original story with fresh insight, and will instruct and challenge you to press on in your own journey, face your own giants and climb your own hills until the day we cross the Final River or are caught up to met our Savoir in the air. In the words of John Bunyan himself, "This book will make a traveller of thee, if by its counsel thou wilt ruled be."

9781926765792 • 118 pages

www.ingramcontent.com/pod-product-compliance
Lightning Source LLC
Chambersburg PA
CBHW070852050426
42453CB00012B/2157